Super Cute
Crispy Treats

ASHLEY FOX WHIPPLE, CREATOR OF *CUTE AS A FOX*

Race Point
PUBLISHING

In memory of my most enthusiastic
taste tester, Kim Bennett.

Race Point Publishing
An imprint of Quarto Publishing Group USA Inc.
142 West 36th Street, 4th Floor
New York, NY 10018

RACE POINT PUBLISHING and the distinctive Race Point Publishing logo
are trademarks of Quarto Publishing Group USA Inc.

ISBN: 978-1-631060-79-3

Photography: Rick Schwab
Food Styling: Janine Kalesis, Lauren LaPenna, and Rick Schwab
Assistant Food Stylist Chantal Lambeth
Art Direction and Prop Styling: Heidi North

Library of Congress Cataloging-in-Publication Data is available

Printed in China

1 3 5 7 9 10 8 6 4 2

www.racepointpub.com

Contents

Chapter Three: Celebrations and Special Occasions 57

Chapter Four: Crispy Shapes 73

Chapter Five: Crispy Treats Squared 95

Chapter Six: Alternative Crispy Treats   135

Introduction

• • , • • • • • • , • •

I love to create art with food. My first real memory of such an endeavor was a seventh-grade science assignment. We had to make a model of an eye, and I talked my group into using cake, frosting, and candies to build ours. I don't remember it turning out terribly professional looking, but we did it. That experience showed me that you can make anything with food if you set your mind to it.

In 2010, I started a craft blog, *Cute as a Fox*. I started blogging because I had created a unique craft that I wanted to tell the whole world about. After focusing on crafts for awhile, I discovered my house was overflowing with cute knick-knacks, and I was running out of people to give gifts to. That was when it dawned on me that I could take my creative inspirations and apply them to food. Food can be cute and clever too! Plus, food gets eaten, so you don't have to worry about it accumulating and collecting dust!

Rice crispy treats are my favorite medium for food art. They are fast and easy to make, malleable, and of course, they taste delicious and lend themselves well to various flavor combinations and enhancements. Some of my very first food art projects involved rice crispy treats, and they are the subjects of some of my most popular blog posts.

Before you get started, please take a moment to read "General Treat Tips" (see page viii). There you will find bits of advice that will help to make your treats not only super cute, but super easy, too. Note that there are several products and terms that I mention throughout the book that you may not be familiar with if you are new to food art; for your convenience, I've provided brief explanations in the glossary on page 164. Should you, your family members, or guests have any dietary restrictions, I've also included a section on ingredient alternatives (see page 166).

I had an absolute ball creating recipes for this book that are not only tasty, but fun and festive. Once that creative switch gets flipped, it is hard to turn it off. I hope you enjoy making and eating these treats as much as I enjoyed creating them for you.

General Treat Tips

- Working with marshmallows can be a highly sticky proposition. It's imperative to grease everything from your hands to the pan you are using to serve them in. I prefer nonstick cooking spray because it is easy to use, it has no real taste, and it doesn't add any calories. You can also use butter or margarine to grease your hands and pans if you prefer. (Greasing with butter is a great hand moisturizer!)

- Some of the treats in the book require that you mold or sculpt the cereal-marshmallow mixture into shapes. You may find that as the treats cool, they become difficult to work with. Just pop your treats in the microwave for 5 to 10 seconds and they will be warm and pliable again.

- Crispy treats are really best when made and eaten within 24 hours. However, when stored in an airtight container, they can last several days. If your treats have gone stale, simply pop them in the microwave for a few seconds and they will be nice and chewy again.

- For treats with frosting, I recommend storing any leftovers covered in the refrigerator. Just give them 20 to 30 minutes on the countertop to warm to room temperature before serving again. Cold crispy treats are brittle and difficult to eat.

- For crispy treat bars, I advise cutting the bars close to the time you are serving them. Once again, treats can get stale over time. That being said, if you are taking a plate of treats to a party, feel free to slice them before you go and keep them in an airtight container or covered with cling wrap or aluminum foil until the time comes to serve them.

- Regarding kitchen equipment to have on hand, the items most utilized to make the recipes include 3-quart (2.8 L) and 5-quart (4.7 L) — or even larger — saucepans; a 9 x 13-inch (22 x 33 cm) baking dish; a serrated knife, for cutting the treats; and a large airtight container for storage.

Buttercream Frosting

YIELD: 3 CUPS (375 G)

½ cup or 1 stick (113 g)
  butter, softened
1½ tsp clear vanilla extract
4 to 6 tbsp milk
4 to 4 ½ (480–540 g) cups
  powdered sugar

Making the frosting: In a large bowl, beat softened butter until creamy with a hand mixer or stand mixer. Beat in vanilla. Add sugar, 1 cup at a time, and beat until incorporated. When frosting becomes too dry, add 1 tablespoon of milk. Alternate between adding milk and sugar until all of both ingredients have been added. If consistency needs to be adjusted, use powdered sugar to thicken and milk to thin. If you're using the buttercream later in the day, place a damp towel over the frosting until you're ready to use (approximately 3–4 hours). Otherwise store the frosting in a covered container in the refrigerator until ready to use, for up to one week.

Coloring the frosting: Unless a large amount of frosting is needed at once, put ½ to 1 cup of frosting in a bowl and color with gel food coloring. Most of the projects in this book call for smaller amounts of frosting.

Storing: Buttercream frosting can be stored in an airtight container in the refrigerator for 1 week. For longer storage, freeze the frosting for up to 3 months. Always let the frosting return to room temperature before using, and lightly beat it to make sure it's light and fluffy.

Buttercream Frosting

Piping the frosting: Buttercream frosting is great for piping details onto cakes and treats. To pipe, you will need a coupler (consisting of a base and a ring), a decorating tip, and a piping bag. I prefer disposable piping bags.

1 Cut approximately 1 inch (2.5 cm) off the tip of the piping bag and insert coupler base so that one thread extends beyond the tip of the bag. Next, place the decorating tip over the exposed portion of coupler base.

2 Screw the coupler ring onto the coupler base (over the decorating tip) from the outside of the bag.

3 Fill piping bag approximately halfway with frosting.
Twist top of bag closed or use a rubber band to secure.

4 Squeeze with even pressure from top of bag to force frosting out the tip. If you are new to piping, practice a few times on a plate or paper towel before decorating your treats.

Chapter One

Crispy Treats
on a Stick

Pinwheel Treats

· · · · ● · ● · ● · ● · ● · ● · ●

Whether they are young kids or just young at heart, guests will love these crispy treat re-creations of the classic children's toy.

YIELD: APPROXIMATELY
12 PINWHEELS
TIME: 1 HOUR ACTIVE,
20 MINUTES DRYING TIME
DIFFICULTY LEVEL: ADVANCED

3 tbsp margarine
1 10-ounce (280 g) bag mini marshmallows
½ cup (85 g) white chocolate chips
6 cups (150 g) crisp rice cereal
Food color spray of your choice
2 ounces (55 g) almond bark
12 small candies (for center of pinwheels)

Equipment: 12 6-inch (15 cm) lollipop sticks or 10-inch (25 cm) wood skewers, paring knife

1   Melt margarine over low heat in a 5-quart or larger saucepan. Add marshmallows, and stir. Let marshmallows melt completely, stirring occasionally. Add white chocolate chips and stir until completely melted. Remove from heat.

2   Stir in crisp rice cereal until covered with marshmallow. Turn out onto a greased baking sheet. With greased hands, press down into a thin, even layer. Make layer as thin as possible while keeping cereal mixture tightly packed. Spray top side of mixture with food color spray. Try to get even coverage.

3   Cut rice cereal mixture into 3½-inch (7.5 cm) squares. Using a paring knife, cut 2- to 2¼-inch (5–5.75 cm) slits in all 4 corners of each square. Before you make the cut, make sure the tip of your knife is pointed directly at the center of the corner that is diagonally opposite from where you're cutting. This will ensure your pinwheel looks even all the way around.

4   Once you've made the slits, each corner will essentially have two separate points. Take one point and fold in toward the center of the square, squishing the point down at the center; leave the second point from that corner as is. Continue to make the rest of the pinwheel by folding up only every other point (in other words, you will alternate between folding one point up and leaving the next point down, as you go around the square). Repeat for the rest of the pinwheels.

5 Using a microwave-safe dish, heat almond bark in microwave in 30-second increments until completely melted, stirring between each heating. (I recommend using High power level for first heating and switching to 50 percent power for subsequent heatings.) Use melted almond bark to attach a small candy to center of each pinwheel.

6 Dip about 1 inch (2.5 cm) of a lollipop stick in almond bark and insert it up through the bottom of pinwheel. Repeat for rest of sticks. Leave treats horizontal, until almond bark has set.

7 Store horizontally in an airtight container on the countertop and serve within 24 hours. Or, to conserve space, layer the pin wheels with wax paper inside the airtight container.

Lollipop Treats

Throwing a candy-themed party? These lollipops look as sweet as candy, but have the welcome taste and satisfying texture of a crispy treat.

YIELD: 16 TO 20 LOLLIPOPS
TIME: 30 MINUTES
DIFFICULTY LEVEL: EASY

3 tbsp margarine
1 10-ounce (280 g) bag mini marshmallows
Gel food coloring in favorite color (optional)
6 cups (150 g) crisp rice cereal
2 ounces (55 g) almond bark,
2 cups (250 g) Buttercream Frosting (see page ix), tinted color of choice

2½-inch circle cookie cutter, 20 lollipop sticks, piping bag, coupler, number 3 tip, cake pop stand or lollipop stand (optional)

1 Melt margarine over low heat in a 5-quart or larger saucepan. Add marshmallows, and stir. Let marshmallows melt completely, stirring occasionally. Remove from heat. For colored crispy treats, add a few drops of gel food coloring and stir to combine. Continue adding gel coloring until desired shade is reached.

2 Stir in crisp rice cereal until covered with marshmallow. Turn out onto a greased baking sheet. With greased hands, press down into an even ½-inch (1.25 cm) thick layer. Cut out circle shapes with cookie cutter.

3 Using a microwave-safe dish, heat almond bark in the microwave in 30-second increments until completely melted, stirring between each heating. (I recommend using High power level for first heating and switching to 50 percent power for subsequent heatings.) Dip one end of a lollipop stick in melted almond bark and insert that end into bottom of lollipop circle. Repeat for rest of pops. Keep lollipops horizontal until almond bark has had time to set. Using a piping bag and number 3 tip, pipe a swirl pattern onto lollipops with buttercream frosting.

4 Store horizontally in the refrigerator in an airtight container or covered with plastic wrap, and serve within 24 hours. Remove from fridge 20 to 30 minutes prior to serving. To serve, display lollipop treats upright in a cake pop stand or lay them horizontally on a platter.

Crispy Root Beer Float Push-Pops

While root beer floats may seem a bit old-fashioned, this crispy treat version is anything but. The root beer extract gives these treats an amazing flavor.

YIELD: 6 PUSH-POPS
TIME: 1¼ HOURS
DIFFICULTY LEVEL: INTERMEDIATE

Rice Cereal Mixture

3 tbsp margarine
1 10-ounce (280 g) bag mini marshmallows
1 tbsp root beer extract
Chocolate-brown gel food coloring (optional)
6 cups (150 g) crisp rice cereal

Frosting

¼ cup or ½ stick butter (57 g), softened
1½ tsp vanilla extract
4 cups (400 g) powdered sugar
4 tbsp milk

9 x 13-inch (22 x 33 cm) baking dish, push-pop containers, circle cookie cutter of the same diameter as or slightly smaller than push-pop container, push-pop stand

1 First make the rice cereal mixture. Melt margarine over low heat in a 5-quart or larger saucepan. Add marshmallows, and stir. Let marshmallows melt completely, stirring occasionally. Stir in root beer extract and remove from heat. If desired, add a few drops of food coloring and stir to incorporate. Continue adding food coloring until desired shade is reached.

2 Pour in crisp rice cereal and stir until covered with marshmallow. Turn out into a greased 9 × 13-inch (22 × 33 cm) baking dish. Press down with greased hands or spatula. Let cool.

3 Next, make the frosting. Beat together softened butter and vanilla extract in a large bowl. Add 1 cup (100 g) of the powdered sugar and 1 tablespoon of the milk. Beat until completely incorporated. Continue adding sugar and milk in this manner until desired consistency is reached (you may not need all of the sugar and milk).

4 Assemble push-pop containers (if not preassembled) and set aside. Cut circles from root beer treat mixture with cookie cutter. Starting with root beer crispy treat, alternate layers of it and vanilla frosting until there are 3 of each. Store covered in the refrigerator a push-pop stand serve within 24 hours. (Due to the awkward shape of the push-pop containers with their sticks, you may want to layer the treats just before serving so you don't have to store them.)

Inside-Out Caramel Apple Crispy Pops

Just like the name suggests, these confections are caramel apples turned inside out: apple cider–flavored treats with the added bonus of a caramel center. If pops are not your thing, forgo the sticks. These treats are just as good when you use your fingers to "pop" them into your mouth!

YIELD: APPROXIMATELY 12 TO 15 POPS
TIME: 1 HOUR
DIFFICULTY LEVEL: INTERMEDIATE

2 tbsp margarine
2¾ cups (5 ounces [140 g]) mini marshmallows
1½ tbsp or 1 individual-serving packet powdered apple cider mix
3 cups (75 g) crisp rice cereal
12 to 15 caramel squares, unwrapped
½ cup (60 g) caramel bits
1 tsp water

Equipment: 15 lollipop sticks, cake pop or lollipop stand, 15 2 x 3-inch (5 cm x 7.5 cm) clear plastic treat bags

1 Melt margarine over low heat in a 3-quart or larger saucepan. Add marshmallows, and stir. Let marshmallows melt completely, stirring occasionally. Add apple cider mix and stir until incorporated. Remove from heat.

2 Pour in crisp rice cereal and stir until covered with marshmallow. If necessary, allow mixture to cool for a few minutes. With well-greased hands, take a handful of mixture and form a patty approximately 2 inches (5 cm) in diameter. Place a caramel square at center and form tight ball around it. Insert lollipop stick about halfway into treat, so that it's stuck into the caramel square at center. Repeat to make rest of pops.

3 Using a microwave-safe dish, heat caramel bits and water in the microwave in 30-second increments until completely melted and smooth, stirring between each heating. (I suggest trying High power level for first heating and switching to 50 percent power for subsequent heatings.) Drizzle over treats. Reheat caramel as necessary, as it cools very quickly. Let treats cool in a cake pop or lollipop stand.

4 After pops are dry, place each in its own clear plastic treat bag and secure with a twist tie. Store at room temperature and serve within 24 hours.

Dipped Crispy Pops

Dipped crispy pops are a refreshing twist on the ever-popular cake pop. This no-bake alternative is easier to execute, but still elicits "oohs" and "aahs" from the crowd.

YIELD: APPROXIMATELY 30 POPS
TIME: 1 HOUR ACTIVE,
40 MINUTES DRYING TIME
DIFFICULTY LEVEL: INTERMEDIATE

3 tbsp margarine
1 10-ounce (240 g) bag
   mini marshmallows
6 cups (150 g) crisp
   rice cereal
1 pound (455 g) almond bark
Sprinkles, sanding sugar,
   or other small toppings

Equipment: 30 lollipop sticks, cake pop or lollipop stand, 30 2 x 3-inch (5 cm x 7.5 cm) clear plastic treat bags

1   Melt margarine over low heat in a 5-quart or larger saucepan. Add marshmallows, and stir. Let marshmallows melt completely, stirring occasionally. Remove from heat.

2   Stir in crisp rice cereal until covered with marshmallow. As soon as mixture is cool enough to handle, form into 1-inch (2.5 cm) balls with greased hands. Set balls on a greased baking sheet or parchment paper. Allow to cool completely.

3   Using a microwave-safe dish, heat 2 ounces (55 g) of the almond bark in the microwave in 30-second increments until completely melted, stirring between each heating. Dip one end of a lollipop stick into melted almond bark, then insert stick into a crispy treat ball. Repeat for all of treats. Allow almond bark to set completely before moving on.

4   Place 6 ounces (170 g) of the almond bark in a short microwave-safe glass and heat in microwave in 30-second increments, until completely melted. Dip one crispy pop at a time in almond bark, gently shaking off any excess. Turn pop upright and immediately add any sprinkles, sanding sugar, or other toppings, then place upright in cake pop or lollipop stand. Melt additional almond bark as needed. Dip all pops and allow to dry completely.

5   After pops are dry, place each in its own clear plastic treat bag and secure with a twist tie. Serve within 24 hours.

Watermelon Treats

Not only do these look like real watermelon slices, they taste like them too!

YIELD: 12 WATERMELON SLICES
TIME: 40 MINUTES ACTIVE,
20 MINUTES COOLING
DIFFICULTY LEVEL: EASY

4 tbsp margarine

1 10-ounce (280 g) bag
mini marshmallows

Green gel food coloring

6 cups (150 g) crisp
rice cereal

½ tsp watermelon
powdered drink mix

Red gel food coloring,
if needed

¼ cup (45 g) mini chocolate
chips

Equipment: 2 9-inch
(22 cm) round baking
pans, 12 miniature ice-pop
sticks (optional)

1 Melt 2 tablespoons of the margarine over low heat in a 3-quart or larger saucepan. Add half of the marshmallows (2¾ cups [140 g]) and stir. Let marshmallows melt completely, stirring occasionally. Remove from heat. Add a few drops of green gel food coloring and stir to combine. Continue adding gel coloring until desired shade is reached.

2 Stir in 3 cups (75 g) of the crisp rice cereal until covered with marshmallow. Divide green mixture between two greased baking dishes, pressing it around the edge of each baking dish with greased hands to form the watermelon rind. Try to make even all the way around. Set aside while you make red layer.

3 Melt remaining margarine over low heat in a 3-quart or larger saucepan. Add remaining marshmallows and stir. Let marshmallows melt completely, stirring occasionally. Add watermelon drink mix and stir. Remove from heat. If necessary, add red gel food coloring, a few drops at a time, until desired shade is reached.

4 Stir in remaining crisp rice cereal until covered with marshmallow. Fill center of each baking dish with red mixture. Press everything down evenly, making sure red and green sections are level with each other. Sprinkle miniature chocolate chips over red section, for watermelon seeds. Gently press chips down into treat mixture. Allow to cool completely.

5 Slice each watermelon treat mixture into 6 even slices. If desired, insert a miniature ice-pop stick into each. Store in an airtight container on countertop and serve within 24 hours.

Paintbrush Crispy Treats

Amuse your budding artist with these fun paintbrush crispy treats. These are perfect for serving at an art-themed or craft-making party.

YIELD: 16 PAINTBRUSH TREATS
TIME: 40 MINUTES ACTIVE.
20 MINUTES DRYING
DIFFICULTY: EASY

3 tbsp margarine
1 10-ounce (280 g) bag
   mini marshmallows
6 cups (150 g) crisp rice cereal
10 ounces (280 g) candy melts,
   divided in assorted colors
   (no single color should be
   less than 2 ounces)

Equipment: 9 x 13-inch
(22 x 33 cm) baking dish,
ice-pop sticks, parchment
paper

1 Melt margarine over low heat in a 5-quart or larger saucepan. Add marshmallows, and stir. Let marshmallows melt completely, stirring occasionally. Remove from heat.

2 Stir in crisp rice cereal until covered with marshmallow. Turn out into a 9 × 13-inch (22 × 33 cm) baking dish and press into an even layer. Cut treat mixture into 2 × 3-inch (5 × 7.5 cm) rectangles. These rectangles will be the brush part of the paintbrushes. Insert an ice-pop stick into each brush.

3 Using a microwave-safe dish, heat candy melts of the same color in the microwave in 30-second increments, until melted, stirring between each heating. Dip the end of the paintbrush that's opposite the stick in the candy melts, but do not shake off excess. Place paintbrush on a sheet of parchment paper, in a standing position. The excess candy melts will pool at bottom of brush and look like paint. Repeat for rest of treats, switching colors of candy melts as desired (if you're using a lot of 1 color in particular, you may need to reheat for appropriate consistency). Let treats set completely before moving.

4 Store in an airtight container on countertop and serve within 24 hours.

Peanut Butter and Jelly Crispy Pops

This recipe was created for my husband and son, who both love PB&J sandwiches.

YIELD: APPROXIMATELY 15 POPS
TIME: 1½ HOURS
DIFFICULTY LEVEL: ADVANCED

2 tbsp margarine
2¾ cups (5 ounces [140 g]) mini marshmallows
⅓ cup (90 g) peanut butter
3 cups (75 g) crisp rice cereal
½ cup (325 g) strawberry or grape jelly
2 ounces (50 g) almond bark
Optional: additional ½ cup jelly

Equipment: Parchment paper, lollipop sticks, cake pop or lollipop stand (optional)

1 Melt margarine over low heat in a 3-quart or larger saucepan. Add marshmallows, and stir. Let marshmallows melt completely, stirring occasionally. Add peanut butter and stir until completely incorporated. Remove from heat.

2 Pour in crisp rice cereal and stir until covered with marshmallow. If necessary, allow mixture to cool a few minutes. With well-greased hands, take a handful of mixture and form a patty approximately 2 inches (5 cm) in diameter. Place approximately 1 teaspoon of jelly in center of patty and form a tight ball around it. Repeat to make rest of treats. Let cool on parchment paper.

3 Using a microwave-safe bowl, heat almond bark in the microwave in 30-second increments until completely melted, stirring between each heating. (I recommend using High power level for first heating and switching to 50 percent power for subsequent heatings.) Dip one end of a lollipop stick in almond bark and carefully insert stick into a peanut butter–jelly ball, so stick is facing up. Allow almond bark to set completely.

4 Optional: In a small saucepan, heat ½ cup (160 g) jelly until melted and a sauce forms. Drizzle over pops. Let cool in a cake pop or lollipop stand.

5 Store in an airtight container or cover with plastic wrap. Refrigerate if not serving within a few hours, but let pops sit at room temperature for at least 10 minutes before serving. Enjoy within 24 hours.

Candied Apple Crispy Treats

• • • • • • • • • • • • •

Do you remember eating candied apples at the local fair? These crispy treat versions are just as wonderfully gooey and sticky as the original.

YIELD: 16 TO 20 TREATS
TIME: 1 HOUR ACTIVE.
1½ HOURS DRYING TIME
DIFFICULTY LEVEL: ADVANCED

Rice Cereal Mixture

3 tbsp margarine
1 10-ounce (280 g) bag mini marshmallows
3 tbsp or 2 individual-serving packets powdered apple cider mix
6 cups (150 g) crisp rice cereal
¾ cup (90 g) dried apples, finely chopped

Candy Coating

2 cups (400 g) sugar
1 cup (300 g) corn syrup
1½ cups (355 ml) water
8 drops red gel food coloring or ½ 0.14-ounce (3.9 g) packet red-colored Kool-Aid

Equipment: Parchment paper, 20 lollipop sticks, sugar thermometer

1 Melt margarine over low heat in a 5-quart or larger saucepan. Add marshmallows, and stir. Let marshmallows melt completely, stirring occasionally. Mix in apple cider powder. Remove from heat.

2 Pour in crisp rice cereal and stir until covered with marshmallow. Fold in dried apples. Let sit for 5 minutes. With well-greased hands, take a handful of mixture and form into an apple shape, packing it tightly. Repeat for rest of cereal mixture. Place apple treats on a sheet of parchment paper. Insert lollipop sticks into base of apple treats and transfer to freezer for at least 1 hour.

3 Next make the candy coating. Pour sugar, corn syrup, and water in a saucepan and stir a few times to combine. Heat mixture on medium-high heat until sugar reaches 300 to 310°F (150–160°C) on a sugar thermometer. Do not stir while mixture is boiling. Remove from heat and stir in red food coloring or, for added flavor, Kool-Aid.

4 Working as quickly as possible, dip each apple treat in candy coating and place on a greased baking sheet with lollipop stick pointing up. Let sit until candy coating has set completely. Loosely cover with plastic wrap until ready to serve. Serve within 24 hours.

Sparkling Star Princess Wands

Highly versatile, they not only make for an enchanting dessert, but can also serve as table decorations and party favors.

YIELD: APPROXIMATELY 15 WANDS
TIME: 45 MINUTES
DIFFICULTY LEVEL: EASY

3 tbsp margarine
1 10-ounce (280 g) bag mini marshmallows
Gel food coloring of choice
6 cups (150 g) crisp rice cereal
Disco dust
2 ounces (55 g) almond bark, melted (optional)

Equipment: 9 x 13-inch (22 x 33 cm) baking dish, 2½–3 inch (6–7.5 cm) star cookie cutter, parchment paper (optional), 15 striped paper straws

Treat Tip:

To use wands as party favors, cover stars with clear treat bags and secure with a twist tie or ribbon.

1 Melt margarine over low heat in a 5-quart or larger saucepan. Add marshmallows, and stir. Let marshmallows melt completely, stirring occasionally. Remove from heat. Add a few drops of food coloring and stir to incorporate. Continue adding food coloring until desired shade is reached.

2 Pour in crisp rice cereal and stir until covered with marshmallow. Turn out into a well-greased 9 × 13-inch (22 × 33 cm) baking dish. With greased hands or spatula, press mixture into an even layer. Let cool.

3 Cut out stars from mixture with cookie cutter. Set on a sheet of parchment paper or a baking sheet that has been coated with nonstick cooking spray.

4 Sprinkle disco dust over star treats until desired amount of shimmer is attained. Gently insert paper straw into bottom of each star. (For maximum security, you can dip the end of each paper straw into melted almond bark before inserting into the star.)

5 Store at room temperature in an airtight container, and serve within 24 hours.

Mustache Treats

Nothing brings a smile to the faces of both children and adults like a fake mustache. These mustache-shaped treats make for a great photo opportunity, as well as being a delicious dessert.

YIELD: 9 MUSTACHES
TIME: 45 MINUTES ACTIVE.
20 MINUTES DRYING TIME
DIFFICULTY LEVEL: INTERMEDIATE

3 tbsp margarine
1 10-ounce (280 g) bag mini marshmallows
6 cups (150 g) chocolate crisp rice cereal
2 ounces (55 g) almond bark
2 cups (250 g) chocolate frosting or Buttercream Frosting (page ix), tinted brown (optional)

Equipment: 9 x 13-inch (22 x 33 cm) baking dish, 4-inch (10 cm) long mustache cookie cutter, 9 lollipop sticks, piping bag (optional), coupler (optional) number 8 icing tip (optional)

1 Melt margarine over low heat in a 5-quart or larger saucepan. Add marshmallows, and stir. Let marshmallows melt completely, stirring occasionally. Remove from heat.

2 Stir in chocolate crisp rice cereal until covered with marshmallow. Turn out into a 9 × 13-inch (22 × 33 cm) baking dish and press into an even layer. Let cool.

3 Cut out mustaches from treat mixture with cookie cutter and set aside.

4 Using a microwave-safe dish, heat almond bark in the microwave in 30-second increments until melted, stirring between each heating. (I recommend using High power level for first heating and switching to 50 percent power for subsequent heatings.) Dip end of a lollipop stick into melted almond bark and insert it into center of mustache. Leave mustache as is, or pipe some lines onto it with a number 8 tip. Keep mustaches horizontal until almond bark has had time to set.

5 Store in an airtight container (in the refrigerator if treats have frosting) and serve within 24 hours.

Peanut Butter Cup Crispy Pops

● ● ● ● ● ● ● ● ● ● ● ● ● ● ●

Peanut butter paired with chocolate is a match made in heaven. Friends and family will be thrilled to bite into these chocolate-covered crispy pops and find a mini peanut butter cup nestled in the center.

YIELD: APPROXIMATELY 20 POPS
TIME: 1½ HOURS
DIFFICULTY LEVEL: ADVANCED

2 tbsp margarine
2¾ cups (5 ounces [140 g]) mini marshmallows
⅓ cup (90 g) peanut butter
4 cups (100 g) crisp rice cereal
20 mini peanut butter cups
4 ounces (115 g) chocolate almond bark

20 lollipop sticks, 20 2 x 3-inch (5 cm x 7.5 cm) clear plastic treat bags

1 Melt margarine over low heat in a 3-quart or larger saucepan. Add marshmallows, and stir. Let marshmallows melt completely, stirring occasionally. Add peanut butter and stir until completely incorporated. Remove from heat.

2 Pour in crisp rice cereal and stir until covered with marshmallow. If necessary, allow to cool a few minutes. With well-greased hands, take a handful of mixture and form a patty approximately 2 inches (5 cm) in diameter. Place 1 peanut butter cup in center and form a tight ball around it. Repeat for rest of treat mixture.

3 Using a microwave-safe dish, heat 2 ounces (55 g) chocolate almond bark in the microwave in 30-second increments until completely melted, stirring between each heating. (I recommend using High power level for first heating and switching to 50 percent power for subsequent heatings.)

4 Dip one end of a lollipop stick into melted almond bark, then insert into a peanut butter treat. Repeat to make rest of pops.

5 Melt the remaining almond bark in the manner described in step 2. Drizzle over pops and let cool in a cake pop or lollipop stand. After pops are dry, place each in its own clear plastic treat bag and secure with a twist tie. Store at room temperature and serve within 24 hours.

Chapter Two

Holidays and Seasons

Coconut Snowballs

Dipped and rolled in coconut, these treats are perfect for a winter-themed party—or simply anytime you have a coconut craving.

YIELD: APPROXIMATELY 18 SNOWBALLS
TIME: 1 HOUR
DIFFICULTY LEVEL: INTERMEDIATE

2 tbsp coconut oil
2¾ cups (5 ounces [140 g]) mini marshmallows
3 cups (75 g) crisp rice cereal
1½ cups (280 g) sweetened flaked coconut
16 ounces (455 g) almond bark

Equipment: Parchment paper

1 Heat coconut oil in a 3-quart or larger saucepan over low heat. Add marshmallows, and stir. Let marshmallows melt completely, stirring occasionally. Remove from heat. Pour in rice cereal and stir until covered with marshmallow.

2 With greased hands, form rice cereal mixture into balls that are 1 to 2 inches (2.5–5 cm) in diameter, and place them on a greased baking sheet. Let cool.

3 Place coconut flakes in a shallow bowl and keep at the ready.

4 Using a microwave-safe mug, heat half of the almond bark in the microwave in 30-second increments until completely melted, stirring between each heating. (I recommend using High power level for first heating and switching to 50 percent for subsequent heatings.) Insert a toothpick into a treat and dip into the melted almond bark. Gently shake off any excess almond. Next, place dipped treat in the bowl of flaked coconut, removing the toothpick at the same time. Sprinkle some coconut on top and gently roll the ball around to coat completely. Move snowball to a sheet of parchment paper and allow to set. Repeat with all treats. Melt additional almond bark as needed.

Gingerbread People Treats

Decorating gingerbread people is a great family holiday tradition. Skip the stress and mess of baking, and make these easy treats instead.

YIELD: 6 GINGERBREAD PEOPLE
TIME: 30 MINUTES, PLUS DECORATING TIME
DIFFICULTY LEVEL: EASY

3 tbsp margarine
1 10-ounce (280 g) bag mini marshmallows
½ tsp ground ginger
½ tsp ground cinnamon
¼ tsp ground cloves
Brown gel food coloring
6 cups (150 g) crisp rice cereal
2 cups (250 g) white Buttercream Frosting (see page ix)
Various candies for decorating

Equipment: 5-inch (12.75 cm) gingerbread person cookie cutter

1 Melt margarine over low heat in a 5-quart or larger saucepan. Add marshmallows, and stir. Let marshmallows melt completely, stirring occasionally. Stir in ginger, cinnamon, and cloves. Remove from heat. Add brown gel food coloring and stir to combine. Continue adding food coloring until desired shade is reached.

2 Stir in crisp rice cereal until completely covered with marshmallow. Turn out onto a greased baking sheet. With greased hands, press down into an even ½-inch (1.25 cm) thick layer. Cut out gingerbread people with cookie cutter.

3 Add facial features, clothes, and anything else you can think of using frosting and candy.

4 Store in an airtight container in the refrigerator and serve within 24 hours.

Tip Treat:
Gingerbread people cutters come in lots of different sizes, but keep in mind that it will be easiest to add details to a large gingerbread person.

Snowflake Treats

It is said that no two snowflakes look alike, so don't feel that you need to decorate these crispy treat versions uniformly. Adorning these is a great activity to do with kids when cooped up inside on a cold day.

YIELD: APPROXIMATELY 16 SNOWFLAKES
TIME: 40 MINUTES ACTIVE, PLUS DECORATING TIME
DIFFICULTY LEVEL: EASY

3 tbsp margarine or coconut oil

1 10-ounce (280 g) bag mini marshmallows

½ cup (90 g) white chocolate chips

White gel food coloring

6 cups (150 g) crisp rice cereal

2 cups (250 g) Buttercream Frosting (see page ix)

Blue food coloring

Green food coloring

White pearl nonpareils

Blue rainbow disco dust

Equipment: 3-inch (7.5 cm) snowflake cookie cutter, piping bag, coupler, number 5 decorating tip

1 Melt margarine or heat coconut oil in a 5-quart or larger saucepan over low heat. Add marshmallows, and stir. Let marshmallows melt completely, stirring occasionally. Add white chocolate chips and stir until melted. Remove from heat. Stir in a few drops of white gel food coloring.

2 Pour in rice cereal and mix until covered with marshmallow. Turn out onto a greased baking sheet. With greased hands, press mixture down into a layer that is ½ inch (1.25 cm) thick. Let cool completely.

3 Cut snowflake shapes out of mixture with greased cookie cutter.

4 Tint about 1 cup (125 g) of Buttercream Frosting with 5 drops blue and 1 drop green food coloring. This will result in a turquoise color.

5 Using a piping bag and decorating tip, pipe different designs and lines on the snowflake treats. Press white pearl nonpareils into the frosting at the tips, line intersections, and anywhere else you would like. Be creative. Lightly sprinkle disco dust over the finished treats to give them a wintery sheen.

6 Store in an airtight container in the refrigerator and serve within 24 hours.

Santa Hat Treats

Have a holly-jolly Christmas party by serving up these festive Santa hats.

YIELD: 12 TO 15 SANTA HATS
TIME: 1 HOUR ACTIVE,
30 MINUTES DRYING TIME
DIFFICULTY LEVEL: EASY

2 tbsp margarine
2¾ cups (5 ounces [140 g])
    mini marshmallows
Red gel food coloring
3 cups (75 g) crisp rice cereal
6 ounces (170 g) almond bark
½ cup white sanding sugar
Small pearl candies,
    gumballs, or white quins

Equipment: Parchment
paper

Variation:
To create a Santa hat with a bent tip, gently bend the top portion over to the side while forming the hat. Instead of using a pearl candy, attach a white quin to the tip with melted almond bark.

1 Melt margarine over low heat in a 3-quart or larger saucepan. Add marshmallows, and stir. Let marshmallows melt completely, stirring occasionally. Remove from heat. Add red gel food coloring and stir to combine. Continue adding gel coloring until desired shade is reached.

2 Stir in crisp rice cereal until completely covered with marshmallow. As soon as mixture is cool enough to handle, form a small handful into a cone shape for Santa hat. Repeat with rest of cereal mixture.

3 Using a microwave-safe dish, heat almond bark in the microwave in 30-second increments until completely melted, stirring between each heating. (I recommend using High power level for first heating and switching to 50 percent power for subsequent heatings.) Dip the base of a hat into almond bark and gently shake off any excess. Immediately dip same base into sanding sugar to create white rim of hat, then place on parchment paper. With your finger, gently push down top of hat to make a base to hold the pearl candy. Place a small amount of almond bark on top of hat and push candy down into place. Let almond bark dry completely. Repeat for rest of hats. Store in an airtight container and serve within 24 hours.

Snowman Face Treats

Instead of bundling up to build a snowman outdoors, try making these snowman faces in the comfort of your own warm home.

YIELD: 16 SNOWMAN FACES
TIME: 45 MINUTES ACTIVE,
30 MINUTES DRYING TIME
DIFFICULTY LEVEL: EASY

3 tbsp margarine

1 10-ounce (280 g) bag mini marshmallows

6 cups (150 g) crisp rice cereal

8 ounces (225 g) white almond bark

32 candy eyes

16 orange sour tear-shaped candy

Black candy writer

Equipment: 2½-inch (6 cm) circle cookie cutter, parchment paper

1   Melt margarine over low heat in a 5-quart or larger saucepan. Add marshmallows, and stir. Let marshmallows melt completely, stirring occasionally. Remove from heat.

2   Stir in crisp rice cereal until covered with marshmallow. Turn out onto a greased baking sheet. With greased hands press down into an even ½-inch (1.25 cm) thick layer. Let cool completely.

3   Cut out circles of cooled treat mixture with cookie cutter.

4   In a small, microwave-safe dish, heat almond bark in the microwave in 30-second increments until completely melted, stirring between each heating. (I recommend using High power level for first heating and switching to 50 percent power for subsequent heatings.)

5   Dip top of each snowman face into almond bark and gently shake off any excess. Set treats on a sheet of parchment paper. For each, immediately add candy eyes and an orange tear-shaped candy "nose," and use candy writer to make dots in the form of a mouth. Let almond bark set completely.

6   Store in an airtight container on countertop and serve within 24 hours.

Hot Cocoa Reindeer Treats

These reindeer treats are almost too cute to eat. Almost.

YIELD: APPROXIMATELY 6 REINDEER
TIME: 1 HOUR
DIFFICULTY LEVEL: ADVANCED

6 pretzel twists
15 pretzel sticks
2 tbsp margarine
2¾ cups (5 ounces [140 g]) mini marshmallows
1 1-ounce (28 g) packet hot cocoa mix
3 cups (75 g) chocolate crisp rice cereal
4 ounces (115 g) chocolate almond bark
Small candies for eyes and nose

Variation:
For a slightly different look, dip the pretzel sticks in chocolate almond bark before you begin. This will give the legs a darker, smooth look.

1 Use a serrated knife to cut the pretzel twists in half for the antlers. Break pretzel sticks in half for reindeer legs and necks. Set aside.

2 Melt margarine over low heat in a 3-quart or larger saucepan. Add marshmallows, and stir. Let marshmallows melt completely, stirring occasionally. Stir in cocoa mix powder. Remove from heat.

3 Add chocolate crisp rice cereal and stir until completely covered with marshmallow. As soon as mixture is cool enough to handle, begin to form reindeer. For each, sculpt a small round ball for the head and a larger, more elongated shape for the body.

4 Using a microwave-safe dish, heat almond bark in microwave in 30-second increments until completely melted, stirring between each heating. (I recommend using High power level for first heating and switching to 50 percent power for subsequent heatings.) Gently press the pretzel antlers into each side of the heads. Use melted almond bark to affix the pretzel antlers and candy eyes and noses.

5 Insert 4 of the halved pretzel sticks into a reindeer body for legs and stand body up. Insert 1 of the halved sticks into the front of the body and gently slide head onto it, leaving some of the pretzel visible. If head is unsteady, secure pretzel to body and head with melted almond bark. Repeat for the rest of the reindeer. Store in an airtight container on countertop and serve within 24 hours.

Cupid's Heart Treats

Capture the heart of your special someone with a homemade batch of these TLC-filled delights. Make them a day ahead and store in an airtight container.

YIELD: APPROXIMATELY 9 HEARTS
TIME: 1 HOUR
DIFFICULTY LEVEL: INTERMEDIATE

Red Treats

3 tbsp margarine
1 10-ounce (280 g) bag
    mini marshmallows
Red gel food coloring
6 cups (150 g) crisp
    rice cereal

White Treats

2 tbsp margarine
2¾ cups (5 ounces [140 g])
    mini marshmallows
Bright white gel food
    coloring
3 cups (75 g) crisp rice
    cereal

Equipment: 3½-inch (8.75 cm) heart cookie cutter, 1½-inch (3.75 cm) heart cookie cutter, 9 10-inch (25 cm) wood skewers, optional

1 First make the red treats. Melt margarine in a 5-quart or larger saucepan over low heat. Add marshmallows, and stir. Let marshmallows melt completely, stirring occasionally. Remove from heat. Add a few drops of red gel food coloring and stir to combine. Continue adding food coloring until desired shade is attained.

2 Pour in rice cereal and mix until covered with marshmallow. Turn out onto a greased baking sheet. With greased hands, press mixture down into a ½-inch (1.25 cm) thick layer. Let cool completely.

3 Next make the white treats. Repeat steps 1 and 2 using a 3-quart or larger saucepan and the ingredients for the white treats (add only a few drops of white food coloring since it is runny). This will make a half batch.

4 Using the larger heart cookie cutter, cut a heart out of the red treat mixture. With the smaller cutter, cut a heart shape out of the center of the red heart. Set small red heart aside. Cut a small heart from the white treat mixture and gently place it in the middle of the large red heart. Repeat to make the rest of the nested hearts.

5 If you use the wooden skewers, push the pointy end through the nested hearts on a diagonal. Skewer should extend around 1 inch (2.5cm) on each side; cut off any extra. Add a small red heart (point first) to form the tail of the arrow. Cut a small triangle from the scrap treats and add to the pointed end to form the tip of the arrow. Repeat for the rest of the treats if desired.

Rosebud Treats

• • • • • • • • • • • • • •

Sweets and flowers are great gifts, so why not combine the two and create a sugary bloom bouquet?

YIELD: 12 ROSEBUDS
TIME: 1 HOUR ACTIVE,
20 MINUTES DRYING TIME
DIFFICULTY LEVEL: INTERMEDIATE

2 tbsp margarine
2¾ cups (5 ounces [140 g])
    mini marshmallows
Red gel food coloring
3 cups (75 g) crisp rice cereal
Small amount of frosting or
    melted almond bark
24 mint leaves, washed and dried

Equipment: Small and medium circle cookie cutters (approximately 1½ [3.75 cm] and 2¼ [5.75 cm]) inches, green plastic lollipop sticks

Treat Tip:
The mint leaves will wilt after several hours, so don't add them until it's almost time to serve the rosebuds. You can also make the rosebud leaves out of fondant, if you prefer.

1 Melt margarine over low heat in a 3-quart or larger saucepan. Add marshmallows, and stir. Let marshmallows melt completely, stirring occasionally. Remove from heat. Add a few drops of red gel food coloring and stir to combine. Continue adding gel coloring until desired shade of red is attained.

2 Stir in rice cereal until covered with marshmallow. Turn out onto a greased baking sheet. With greased hands, press down into a thin even layer. For every rosebud, cut 1 small circle and 1 medium circle.

3 To form the center of a rosebud, dip one end of a lollipop stick into the frosting or melted almond bark. Roll one of the small circle treats around coated end of lollipop stick with the stick toward the bottom of the treat as the "stem." Press bottom of circle tightly around stick.

4 Next, cut one of the medium circles in half, and using your palms, press down on both halves to flatten slightly. Wrap resulting two semicircles around the part of the rosebud you've already made, starting from opposite sides. Press bottom of the circles tightly to bottom of the central part of the rosebud so that everything sticks together.

5 Shortly before serving, add a small dab of frosting or melted almond bark to 2 mint leaves and press them onto either side of the rosebud. Keep rosebud horizontal until frosting/almond bark dries.

6 Repeat steps 3 through 5 to make the rest of the rosebuds.

Rainbow-Wrapped Shamrock Treats

Inject a bit of whimsy into your St. Patrick's Day celebration with these festive treats.

YIELD: 16 TREATS
TIME: 1 HOUR ACTIVE,
20 MINUTES DRYING TIME
DIFFICULTY LEVEL: EASY

3 tbsp margarine
1 10-ounce (280 g) bag
   mini marshmallows
Green gel food coloring
6 cups (150 g) crisp rice cereal
4 ounces (115 g) almond bark
16 rainbow sour belts

Equipment: 3-inch
shamrock-shaped cookie
cutter, 9 x 13-inch
(22 x 33 cm) baking dish

1 Melt margarine over low heat in a 5-quart or larger saucepan. Add marshmallows, and stir. Let marshmallows melt completely, stirring occasionally. Remove from heat. Add a few drops of green gel food coloring and stir to incorporate. Continue adding food coloring, a few drops at a time, until desired shade is reached.

2 Stir in crisp rice cereal until covered with marshmallow. Turn out into a greased 9 × 13-inch (22 × 33 cm) baking dish. With greased hands, press down into an even layer. Cut out shamrock shapes with cookie cutter.

3 Using a microwave-safe dish, heat almond bark in microwave in 30-second increments until completely melted, stirring between each heating. (I recommend using High power level for first heating and switching to 50 percent power for subsequent heatings.) Place small amount of almond bark on the end of a sour belt and press candy onto edge of a shamrock treat at the base of the leaf where it meets the stem. Wrap sour belt around shamrock leaf, adding almond bark to the sour belt as you go. Finish wrapping on other side of clover leaf. (Note that the sour belt is not long enough to wrap around the stem.) Let almond bark harden. Repeat for all treats.

4 Store in an airtight container on countertop and serve within 24 hours.

Leprechaun Top Hat Treats

These fanciful treats are another great addition to a St. Patrick's Day party.

YIELD: 12 TO 15 TREATS
TIME: 45 MINUTES
DIFFICULTY LEVEL: EASY

3 tbsp margarine
1 10-ounce (280 g) bag
   mini marshmallows
Leaf green gel food coloring
6 cups (150 g) crisp rice cereal
6 rainbow sour belts
2 ounces (55 g) white
   almond bark
Yellow jumbo quins
Green food coloring marker

Equipment: 3-inch (7.5 cm) top
hat cookie cutter (optional)

1 Melt margarine over low heat in a 5-quart or larger saucepan. Add marshmallows, and stir. Let marshmallows melt completely, stirring occasionally. Remove from heat. Add a few drops of green gel food coloring and stir to incorporate. Continue adding food coloring until desired shade is reached.

2 Stir in crisp rice cereal until covered with marshmallow. Turn out onto a greased baking sheet. With greased hands, press down into an even ½-inch (1.25 cm) thick layer. Cut out hat shapes with a cookie cutter or do it freehand using a serrated knife.

3 Cut rainbow sour belts to appropriate length to serve as brims for hats.

4 Using a microwave-safe dish, heat almond bark in the microwave in 30-second increments until completely melted, stirring between each heating. (I recommend using High power level for first heating and switching to 50 percent power for subsequent heatings.) Secure each sour belt brim to each hat with a little melted almond bark. Draw a small shamrock on the yellow quins with the green food marker. Attach each quin to the center of a sour belt brim with the melted almond bark.

5 Store top hats in an airtight container and serve within 24 hours.

Easter Carrot Treats

You won't have to worry about a little bunny coming along and digging up these carrots. Serving them in a "dirt" cup provides an extra special treat.

YIELD: 12 TREATS
TIME: 45 MINUTES FOR CARROTS, PLUS 20 MINUTES TO ASSEMBLE
DIFFICULTY LEVEL: EASY

1-ounce bag (28 g) edible Easter grass
2 tbsp margarine
2¾ cups (5 ounces [140 g]) mini marshmallows
Orange gel food coloring
3 cups (75 g) crisp rice cereal
3 to 4 cups (300 to 400 g) crumbled chocolate cake, brownies, or cookies, for "dirt"

Equipment: 12 8-ounce (237 ml) clear plastic cups

Variation:

If you prefer, you can use ⅓ cup of chocolate pudding for the dirt in each cup. Make sure not to put the carrots in the pudding until right before serving so that they stay nice and crispy.

1 Cut edible Easter grass into pieces that are 2 to 3 inches (5–7.5 cm) in length. Cut about 60 pieces total. Set aside.

2 Melt margarine over low heat in a 3-quart or larger saucepan. Add marshmallows, and stir. Let marshmallows melt completely, stirring occasionally. Remove from heat. Add a few drops of orange gel food coloring and stir to combine. Continue adding food coloring until desired shade is reached.

3 Stir in crisp rice cereal until covered with marshmallow. Once mixture is cool enough to handle, form a small handful into a carrot shape. Cut a slit in the top of the carrot and insert about 5 pieces of Easter grass. Press cereal mixture back together around grass.

4 The "dirt" cups should be assembled right before serving (you can make the carrots up to 24 hours ahead of time and store them in an airtight container on the countertop until ready to assemble). Place each carrot upright in a clear 8-ounce (237 ml) cup. Pack crumbled chocolate cake/brownies/cookies around each carrot. Leave the top of each carrot and its stem exposed.

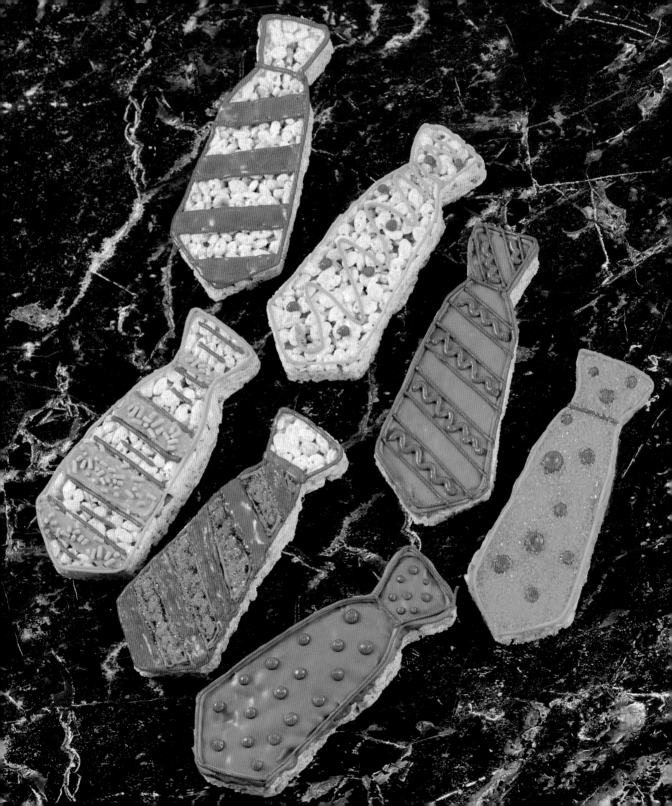

Father's Day Tie Treats

Everyone will have fun decorating these Father's Day ties, and Dad will certainly enjoy eating them. Personalize them with the man of honor's favorite candies or colors to show how much you care.

YIELD: 8 TIES
TIME: 30 MINUTES COOKING TIME,
PLUS DECORATING TIME
DIFFICULTY LEVEL: INTERMEDIATE

3 tbsp margarine
1 10-ounce (280 g) bag
   mini marshmallows
6 cups (150 g) crisp
   rice cereal
2 cups (250 g) Buttercream
   Frosting (see page ix),
   tinted color of choice
Assorted small candies

Equipment: 5-inch (12.75 cm)
long tie cookie cutter

1 Melt margarine in a 5-quart or larger saucepan over low heat. Add marshmallows, and stir. Let marshmallows melt completely, stirring occasionally. Remove from heat.

2 Stir in crisp rice cereal until covered with marshmallow. Turn out onto a greased baking sheet. With greased hands, press down into a ½-inch (1.25 cm) thick layer. Let cool completely. Then cut ties with cookie cutter.

3 Spread a layer of frosting over the treats and decorate with candies.

Tip Treat:
Some decorating ideas you might want to try include using candy polka dots, making stripes with licorice string, or writing a personal message with a gel writer.

Father's Day Trophy Treats

Every dad deserves an award on his special day, so show yours just how much you love him with these trophy treats.

YIELD: 12 TO 15 TROPHIES
TIME: 1 HOUR
DIFFICULTY LEVEL: EASY

3 tbsp margarine
1 10-ounce (280 g) bag mini marshmallows
Yellow gel food coloring
6 cups (150 g) crisp rice cereal
5 feet (1.5 m) yellow licorice string
1 cup (125 g) Buttercream Frosting (see page ix)

Equipment: 4-inch (10 cm) tall wineglass cookie cutter, toothpick

1 Melt margarine in a 5-quart or larger saucepan over low heat. Add marshmallows, and stir. Let marshmallows melt completely, stirring occasionally. Remove from heat. Add yellow gel food coloring and stir to combine. Continue adding gel coloring until desired shade is reached.

2 Stir in crisp rice cereal until covered with marshmallow. Turn out onto a greased baking sheet. With greased hands, press down into an even ½-inch (1.25 cm) thick layer.

3 Cut out treats from cereal mixture with wineglass cookie cutter. Gently press the base of the wineglass-shaped treat up to shorten the stem of the glass. Keep pushing until the wine glass transforms into a trophy.

4 For each trophy treat, cut two 2-inch (5 cm) pieces of yellow licorice string. Next, use a toothpick to make 2 holes on each side of trophy, and insert the licorice strings in the holes for the trophy handles. Press cereal mixture back together around licorice to secure. Decorate with frosting to show your appreciation for Dad.

Alternative:
These trophies would also be perfect for celebrating the end of a great sports season!

Popping Fireworks Treats

Give your guests an extra-special surprise with these fireworks that actually pop in your mouth.

YIELD: 16 TREATS
TIME: 1 HOUR
DIFFICULTY LEVEL: EASY

3 tbsp margarine
1 10-ounce (280 g) bag
  mini marshmallows
6 cups (150 g) crisp rice cereal
2 cups (250 g) Buttercream
  Frosting (see page ix)
8 red licorice strings
8 blue licorice strings
Red and blue star-shaped quins
Red and blue popping candy

Equipment: 2- to 3-inch
(5–7.5 cm) circle cookie cutter

1 Melt margarine in a 5-quart or larger saucepan over low heat. Add marshmallows, and stir. Let marshmallows melt completely, stirring occasionally. Remove from heat.

2 Stir in crisp rice cereal until covered with marshmallow. Turn out onto a greased baking sheet. With greased hands, press down into an even ½-inch (1.25 cm) thick layer. Let cool completely.

3 Cut out circles from treat mixture with cookie cutter. Spread buttercream frosting on each circle. On top of frosting, create a firework burst shape with licorice string; use kitchen shears to taper ends of licorice to make firework look more realistic. Place a star sprinkle in center of each firework and decorate with additional star sprinkles as desired.

4 Store in an airtight container in the refrigerator, and serve within 24 hours. Just before serving, sprinkle fireworks with red and blue popping candy.

Treat Tip:
It's important not to add the popping candy to the fireworks treats until just before serving because it reacts with the air.

American Flag Treat

• • • • • • • • • • • • • •

Display your patriotism with pride! For this recipe, you basically make a full batch of plain crispy treats, a full batch of red treats, and a half batch of blue. And because everything fits in one baking dish, it's easy to transport to a 4th of July barbecue.

YIELD: 24 2-INCH (5 CM) SQUARES
TIME: 1¼ HOURS
DIFFICULTY LEVEL: INTERMEDIATE

8 tbsp margarine
25 ounces (700 g) mini marshmallows
15 cups (375 g) crisp rice cereal
Red gel food coloring
Blue gel food coloring
White star sprinkles

Equipment: 2 9 x 13-inch (22 x 33 cm) baking dishes, 1 8 x 8-inch (20 x 20 cm) baking dish, ruler

Tip Treat:
Use the leftover parts of the crispy treat mixtures to create some stars to serve with your American Flag.

1 Melt 3 tablespoons margarine in a 5-quart or larger saucepan over low heat. Add 1 10-ounce bag marshmallows, and stir. Let marshmallows melt completely, stirring occasionally. Remove from heat.

2 Pour in 6 cups (150 g) crisp rice cereal and stir until covered with marshmallow. Turn out into a greased 9 × 13-inch (22 × 33 cm) baking dish. Set aside and let cool.

3 Repeat step 1, except after removing melted marshmallow from heat, add a few drops of red food coloring and stir to combine. Continue adding red food coloring until desired shade is attained. Then repeat step 2.

4 Melt remaining 2 tablespoons margarine in a 3-quart or larger saucepan. Add 5 ounces (2¾ cups [140 g]) of mini marshmallows, stirring occasionally until melted completely. Remove from heat. Add a few drops of blue food coloring and stir to combine. Continue adding blue food coloring until desired shade is attained.

5 Pour in 3 cups (75 g) crisp rice cereal and stir until covered with marshmallow. Turn out into a greased 8 × 8-inch baking dish. Let cool.

6 Once treat mixtures are cool, turn out onto a cutting board. Using a serrated knife, cut a 5 × 6-inch (12.75 × 15.25 cm) rectangle out of the blue crispy mixture and place in upper

left corner of a clean 9 × 13-inch (22 × 33 cm) baking dish. Cut seven ¾ × 13-inch (2 × 33 cm) stripes out of red crispy mixture, and cut six ¾ × 13-inch (2 × 33 cm) stripes out of plain crispy treat mixture.

7 Starting with a red stripe at bottom of baking dish, alternate adding red and plain crispy treats. A plain stripe should abut the bottom of the blue rectangle, and the final stripe at the top of the baking dish should be red. Trim down the stripes that run alongside blue rectangle as needed. If stripes are a bit too wide, use your fingers to squish them together so that everything fits.

8 Arrange a row of 6 stars, evenly spaced, about ½-inch (1.25 cm) from top of blue rectangle. For the second row, place 5 stars so that they're staggered with the ones in the top row. Continue alternating rows of 6 and 5 stars until you end up with 9 rows total. (The top and bottom rows will each have 6 stars.)

9 Store on countertop in an airtight container or cover with aluminum foil, and serve within 24 hours.

Nutty Acorn Treats

These autumnal treats not only look like acorns, but also have a nice nutty flavor.

YIELD: 12 TO 15 ACORN TREATS
TIME: 40 MINUTES ACTIVE,
20 MINUTES DRYING
DIFFICULTY LEVEL: INTERMEDIATE

2 tbsp margarine
2¾ cups (5 ounces [140 g])
  mini marshmallows
3 cups (75 g) crisp rice cereal
½ cup (85 g) peanut butter
  candy melts
½ cup (60 g) chopped
  nut topping
8 stick pretzels, broken in half

Equipment: Parchment
paper

1 Melt margarine in a 3-quart or larger saucepan over low heat. Add marshmallows, and stir. Let marshmallows melt completely, stirring occasionally. Remove from heat.

2 Stir in crisp rice cereal until covered with marshmallow. As soon as mixture is cool enough to handle, form small handfuls into acorn shapes.

3 Using a microwave-safe dish, heat peanut butter candy melts in the microwave in 30-second increments until completely melted, stirring between each heating. (I recommend using High power level for first heating and switching to 50 percent power for subsequent heatings.) Dip top of an acorn treat in the candy melts and gently shake off any excess. Immediately dip the same end of the acorn into the chopped nut topping. Firmly press a half pretzel into the top of the acorn as a stem. Place the acorn on a sheet of parchment paper to set completely. Repeat for rest of acorn treats.

4 Store in an airtight container on countertop and serve within 24 hours.

Witch Hat Treats

There's no need to cast a spell or brew a secret potion to conjure up delicious treats for Halloween. Friends and family alike are sure to find these witch hats utterly enchanting.

YIELD: 9 HATS
TIME: 45 MINUTES
DIFFICULTY LEVEL: INTERMEDIATE

3 tbsp margarine
1 10-ounce (280 g) bag mini marshmallows
Black gel food coloring
6 cups (150 g) chocolate crisp rice cereal
1 cup (125 g) Buttercream Frosting (see page ix), tinted purple
Halloween-themed candies (optional)

Equipment: 2¼-inch (5.75 cm) circle cookie cutter

1 Melt margarine in a 5-quart or larger saucepan over low heat. Add marshmallows, and stir. Let marshmallows melt completely, stirring occasionally. Remove from heat. Add a few drops of black gel food coloring and stir to combine. Continue adding food coloring until desired shade is reached.

2 Stir in chocolate crisp rice cereal until completely covered with marshmallow. Take half of the mixture and press into an even ½-inch (1.25 cm) thick layer on a greased baking sheet. Use cookie cutter to cut out circles for brims of witch hats. Using the other half of the rice cereal mixture, form tops of witch hats by hand; give the tips a slight bend to the side for added effect.

3 Add purple buttercream frosting to the center of the circles. Use enough so that frosting will be seen after top of each hat is applied. Add tops, pressing them down in middle of frosted area. Leave hats as they are, or add a fun Halloween candy to each as an adornment.

4 Store in an airtight container in the refrigerator, and serve within 24 hours. Remove treats from fridge approximately 20 to 30 minutes before serving.

Spider Treats

These spider treats can be creepy or cute, depending on how you decorate them. The grape flavor guarantees that, no matter how they look, they will be tasty.

YIELD: APPROXIMATELY 10 SPIDERS
TIME: 1 HOUR
DIFFICULTY LEVEL: INTERMEDIATE

2 tbsp margarine

2¾ cups (5 ounces [140 g]) mini marshmallows

½ tsp grape-flavored drink powder mix

Purple gel food coloring (optional)

3 cups (75 g) crisp rice cereal

10 12-inch (30.5 cm) purple licorice strings

4 ounces (115 g) almond bark

20 to 30 small candy eyes

Black candy writer (optional)

Equipment: 1 lollipop stick

1 Melt margarine in a 3-quart or larger saucepan over low heat. Add marshmallows, and stir. Let marshmallows melt completely, stirring occasionally. Add grape drink mix and stir to combine. Remove from heat. For a darker purple color, add purple gel food coloring and stir to combine. Continue adding gel coloring until desired shade is reached.

2 Stir in crisp rice cereal until completely covered with marshmallow. As soon as mixture is cool enough to handle, form a handful into a spider body. Keeping it connected as one piece, form a smaller round head at one end of the body. Repeat to make the rest of the spiders.

3 Cut the purple licorice string into pieces approximately 2 to 2½ inches (5–6 cm) long. Using a lollipop stick, poke 6 holes (3 on each side) into the body of each spider. Insert licorice string pieces into holes and press rice cereal mixture around them to secure.

4 Using a microwave-safe dish, heat almond bark in the microwave in 30-second increments until completely melted, stirring between each heating. (I recommend using High power level for first heating and switching to 50 percent power for subsequent heatings.) Use melted almond bark to attach the eyes to the spider heads. Change it up from spider to spider to give each its own personality. If desired, draw a mouth with a black candy writer.

5 Store in an airtight container and serve within 24 hours.

Truffle-Stuffed Pumpkin Treats

A decadent truffle mixture serves as both a delicious indulgence and a creative decoration here.

YIELD: APPROXIMATELY 10 TREATS
TIME: 1½ HOURS ACTIVE,
1½ HOURS SETTING TIME
DIFFICULTY LEVEL: ADVANCED

1 16-ounce (455 g) package chocolate sandwich cookies

8 ounces (225 g) low-fat cream cheese (Neufchâtel cheese), softened

3 tbsp margarine

1 10-ounce (280 g) bag mini marshmallows

Orange gel food coloring

5 cups (125 g) crisp rice cereal

5 chocolate Tootsie Rolls

¼ cup (56 g) green fondant (optional)

Equipment: Paring knife, small leaf fondant cutter (optional)

1 In a food processor, finely crush chocolate sandwich cookies. Add in softened cream cheese and pulse until completely combined to make the truffle mixture. Using your hands, form a 2-inch (5 cm) ball of the mixture, then gently flatten it into an egg shape. Repeat until you have 10 egg-shaped chocolate truffles. You should have some truffle mix left over, which you will need later on to make the jack-o'-lantern faces. Refrigerate the truffles and leftover mix for 1 hour or until firm.

2 Melt the margarine over low heat in a 5-quart or larger saucepan. Add marshmallows, and stir. Let marshmallows melt completely, stirring occasionally. Remove from heat. Add a few drops of orange food coloring and stir to combine. Continue adding food coloring until desired shade is reached. Pour in crisp rice cereal and stir until covered with marshmallow.

3 Coat clean hands with nonstick cooking spray, butter, or margarine. While cereal mixture is still warm, form a handful into a thin circle or egg shape slightly larger than the truffle. Place a truffle on top of the orange crispy treat. Add more cereal mixture to cover the truffle, sculpting a pumpkin as you go. To make the pumpkin stand up, press it down onto a hard surface to flatten the bottom. Insert half of a Tootsie Roll for the stem, and work cereal

mixture around stem to secure in place. Repeat to form rest of pumpkins. Refrigerate for 30 minutes.

4 With a small paring knife, cut out 2 triangular eyes and a mouth from just the orange layer of each pumpkin treat, so that the truffle center is revealed. Fill in the holes with the leftover truffle mix from step 1. (The easiest way to do this is to sculpt the truffle mix into the appropriate size triangle and mouth shapes before gently pushing it into the holes.)

5 Optional: Roll out green fondant and cut into 10 leaf shapes. Press base of a leaf onto a pumpkin treat right next to the candy stem. Repeat for the rest of the jack-o'-lanterns.

6 Store in an airtight container in the refrigerator. Best if served within 24 hours. Let treats sit out at room temperature for 10 to 15 minutes before serving.

Chapter Three

Celebrations and Special Occasions

Candy-Stuffed Piñata Treats

Wow your guests with these piñata treats. They'll never suspect that there's actually candy stuffed inside, just like the real deal.

YIELD: 6 TO 8 PIÑATAS
TIME: 1¼ HOURS
DIFFICULTY LEVEL: INTERMEDIATE

3 tbsp margarine
1 10-ounce (280 g) bag
  mini marshmallows
6 cups (150 g) Fruity
  Pebbles cereal
1 cup mini chocolate candies
Black candy writer or
  gel writer

Equipment: 3½-inch
(8.75 cm) horse or donkey
cookie cutter

1 Melt margarine in a 5-quart or larger saucepan over low heat. Add marshmallows, and stir. Let marshmallows melt completely, stirring occasionally. Remove from heat.

2 Stir in fruit cereal until covered with marshmallow. Turn out onto a greased baking sheet and press down into a uniform layer. Let cool.

3 For each piñata, cut out 2 donkey shapes with cookie cutter. Place some mini chocolate candies on top of one of the donkey shapes. Place second donkey treat on top of first, then firmly press the two treat layers together at the edges. Repeat to form rest of piñatas.

4 With a candy writer or gel writer, give each donkey an eye and a bridle for some finishing details.

5 Store in an airtight container on countertop, and serve within 24 hours.

Apple-for-Teacher Treats

Start off the school year on the right foot with these cute treats for the teachers in your life. This twist on the classic offering is sure to put a smile on their faces.

YIELD: 8 TO 10 APPLE TREATS
TIME: 1 HOUR
DIFFICULTY LEVEL: INTERMEDIATE

3 tbsp margarine
1 10-ounce (280 g) bag mini marshmallows
Red gel food coloring
6 cups (150 g) crisp rice cereal
Chocolate licorice, pretzel sticks, or Tootsie Rolls, cut into 10 1½-to-2-inch (4–5 cm) pieces
8 to 10 sour gummy worms
¼ cup (56 g) green apple taffy or green fondant
Candy writer (optional)
20 candy eyes (optional)
¼ cup candy melts (optional)

1 Melt margarine over low heat in a 5-quart or larger saucepan. Add marshmallows, and stir. Let marshmallows melt completely, stirring occasionally. Remove from heat. Add a few drops of red gel coloring to marshmallows and stir to incorporate. Continue adding gel coloring until desired shade is reached.

2 Stir in crisp rice cereal until covered with marshmallow. When mixture is cool enough to hold comfortably, with greased hands, form a handful into an apple shape. Place treat on a greased baking sheet. Repeat with rest of cereal mixture.

3 Insert a chocolate licorice piece into the top of each apple treat for a stem. With your finger, make an indentation in the side of each treat for the worm. Insert gummy worm and then reform treat around it if necessary. This step is best performed immediately after the apples are formed, before the treats have had time to set fully.

4 Work green taffy or fondant in your hands to make it malleable. Using kitchen shears, cut taffy into leaf shapes and place one on each apple treat next to the stem.

5 Optional: Use a candy writer to add eyes and mouth to the gummy worms. For the apples, adhere candy eyes with the help of candy melts and draw a mouth with a candy writer.

Onesie Treats

• • • • • • • • • • • • •

For a fun and unique baby shower activity, have guests decorate their own treats. Provide the crispy treats, frosting, sprinkles, and candy, and let those in attendance go to town.

YIELD: APPROXIMATELY 9 ONESIES
TIME: 30 MINUTES, PLUS
DECORATING TIME
DIFFICULTY LEVEL: EASY

3 tbsp margarine

1 10-ounce (280 g) bag mini marshmallows

6 cups (150 g) crisp rice cereal

2 cups (250 g) Buttercream Frosting (see page ix)

Gel food coloring, 2 different colors of your choice

Sprinkles, candy

Equipment: 4-inch (10 cm) long onesie cookie cutter

1   Melt margarine over low heat in a 5-quart or larger saucepan. Add marshmallows, and stir. Let marshmallows melt completely, stirring occasionally. Remove from heat.

2   Stir in crisp rice cereal until covered with marshmallow. Turn out onto a greased baking sheet. With greased hands, press down into an even ½-inch (1.25 cm) thick layer. Cut out onesie shapes with cookie cutter.

3   Divide the frosting in half and tint each half a different color to coordinate with the theme of the baby shower. Decorate onesies with frosting, sprinkles, and candy.

4   Store in an airtight container in the refrigerator and serve within 24 hours.

Gender Reveal Baby Rattles

These charming rattles are a fresh take on the popular gender reveal cake.

YIELD: 8 TO 10 RATTLES
TIME: 1½ HOURS
DIFFICULTY LEVEL: INTERMEDIATE

3 tbsp margarine
1 10-ounce (280 g) bag mini marshmallows
6 cups (150 g) crisp rice cereal
2 ounces (55 g) almond bark
10 white pearl gumballs
1 cup pink or blue chocolate candies
½ cup (62 g) Buttercream Frosting (see page ix), tinted pink
½ cup (62 g) Buttercream Frosting, tinted blue
½ cup (TK g) white Buttercream Frosting (optional)

Equipment: 2½-inch (6 cm) circle cookie cutter, 10 lollipop sticks

1 Melt margarine over low heat in a 5-quart or larger saucepan. Add marshmallows, and stir. Let marshmallows melt completely, stirring occasionally. Remove from heat.

2 Stir in crisp rice cereal until covered with marshmallow. Turn out onto a greased baking sheet. With greased hands, press down into an even ½-inch (1.25 cm) thick layer. Cut out circles with cookie cutter.

3 Using a microwave-safe dish, heat almond bark in microwave in 30-second increments until melted, stirring between each heating. (I recommend using High power level for first heating and switching to 50 percent power for subsequent heatings.) Use a sharp knife to poke a small hole in a gumball that will fit a lollipop stick. Place a bit of melted almond bark on the lollipop stick to help hold it in place; affix gumball. Repeat with rest of the lollipop sticks.

4 Press the other end of a lollipop stick into the edge of one of the circles. Place a small pile of pink or blue chocolate candies, in the center of the circle. Take a second circle and press it on top of the first. Press the edges together to form a good seal around candies. Repeat to form rest of rattles.

5 Decorate top of each rattle with buttercream frosting. Make sure you use both pink and blue to keep the gender a secret until it's time for everyone to take a bite and discover the color hidden inside.

6 Store in an airtight container in the refrigerator and serve within 24 hours.

Graduation Diploma Treats

When celebrating a student's graduation, take the festivities up a notch with these diploma treats. The guest of honor and other attendees are sure to give these high marks.

YIELD: 12 TREATS
TIME: 45 MINUTES
DIFFICULTY LEVEL: EASY

3 tbsp margarine
1 10-ounce (280 g) bag mini marshmallows
6 cups (150 g) crisp rice cereal
8 feet (2.5 m) licorice string
½ cup (62 g) Buttercream Frosting (see page ix) or candy writer (optional)

Equipment (all optional):
Piping bag, coupler, number 2 tip

1 Melt margarine over low heat in a 5-quart or larger saucepan. Add marshmallows, and stir. Let marshmallows melt completely, stirring occasionally. Remove from heat.

2 Pour in crisp rice cereal and stir until covered with marshmallow. Turn out onto a greased baking sheet. With greased hands, press down into an even ½-inch (1.25 cm) thick layer. Cut 2½ × 3½-inch (6 × 8.75 cm) rectangles with a serrated knife.

3 Starting on the longer side, gently roll up each treat to mimic a rolled diploma. Next, tie a piece of licorice string, approximately 8 inches long, around the center of each. You can stop there or write the year on the diploma by piping on frosting or using a candy writer.

Birthday Hat Treats

Who needs cupcakes when you can whip up some birthday hat crispy treats? These festive desserts can easily be coordinated to any party theme by simply changing up the colors.

YIELD: 20 TO 24 TREATS
TIME: 1 HOUR
DIFFICULTY LEVEL: INTERMEDIATE

3 tbsp margarine
1 10-ounce (280 g) bag mini marshmallows
6 cups (150 g) crisp rice cereal
8 ounces (225 g) white almond bark or candy melts
Sanding sugar, optional
24 Sixlets or gumballs
Jumbo quins

1 Melt margarine over low heat in a 5-quart or larger saucepan. Add marshmallows, and stir. Let marshmallows melt completely, stirring occasionally. Remove from heat. Pour in crisp rice cereal and stir until completely incorporated.

2 Coat your hands and a baking sheet with nonstick cooking spray. Take some cereal mixture and form a cone shape approximately 2 inches (5 cm) high. Repeat until all of mixture has been used. Let cones cool completely.

3 Using a microwave-safe dish, heat almond bark in microwave in 30-second increments until completely melted, stirring between each heating. (I recommend using High power level for first heating and switching to 50 percent power for subsequent heatings.) Dip the bottom of a birthday hat in almond bark and gently shake off any excess. Immediately dip bottom of hat into sanding sugar (if using) to create a colorful rim. Place on a greased baking sheet until set. Repeat for all hats.

4 Press a candy ball on the top of each hat, using melted almond bark to adhere ball to treat. Add polka dots to hats by affixing jumbo quins with almond bark. Let almond bark harden. Store in an airtight container on countertop and serve within 24 hours.

Cake Banner Treats

• • •.•.•• •• •.•.•

Banners on cakes have become a popular trend, but you can stand out from the crowd with this edible version.

YIELD: 1 CAKE BANNER
TIME: 1 HOUR
DIFFICULTY LEVEL: ADVANCED

2 tbsp margarine
2¾ cups (5 ounces [140 g])
    mini marshmallows
3 cups (75 g) crisp rice cereal
2 ounces (55 g) almond bark
Candy writer

Equipment: Baker's twine,
2 10-inch (25 cm) long wood
skewers, parchment paper

1   Melt margarine over low heat in a 3-quart or larger saucepan. Add marshmallows, and stir. Let marshmallows melt completely, stirring occasionally. Remove from heat.

2   Stir in crisp rice cereal until covered with marshmallow. Turn out onto a greased baking sheet. With greased hands, press down into an even ½-inch (1.25 cm) thick layer. Allow to cool.

3   Cut baker's twine so that it's 4 inches (10 cm) longer than desired length of banner. Tie one end to top of one of the skewers. Set aside. With a serrated knife, cut triangular pennant shapes from rice cereal mixture. Each pennant should be about 1-inch (2.5 cm) at the top edge. (For longer names, try increasing top edge to about 1½ inches [3.75 cm] and add multiple letters per pennant.) Next, cut a notch into the middle of the top edge of each pennant (the edge from which the pennant will be hung). Set aside.

4   Using a microwave-safe dish, heat almond bark in microwave in 30-second increments until completely melted, stirring between each heating. (I recommend using High power level for first heating and switching to 50 percent power for subsequent heatings.) Place a bit of almond bark inside the notch of one of the pennants, then insert the baker's twine into the notch. Press top of pennant back together around twine. Repeat with all of the pennants, placing them directly next to each other on the twine.

5 Tie the twine at end of banner around top of second skewer. Trim any excess twine. Lay banner down flat on a piece of parchment paper. Using a candy writer, inscribe your message on banner. Leave flat until almond bark has hardened.

6 Wait until just before the cake is put out to add banner. Gently insert skewers into each end of cake. I recommend placing the ends of the skewers at a slight angle toward the center of the cake (see photograph).

Engagement Ring Treats

• • • • • • • • • • • •

Celebrate the happy couple with some sweet and sparkly engagement rings. These elegant treats make great favors for a shower or engagement party.

YIELD: 12 RINGS
TIME: 1½ HOURS
DIFFICULTY LEVEL: ADVANCED

3 tbsp margarine
1 10-ounce (280 g) bag mini marshmallows
6 cups (150 g) crisp rice cereal
Cornstarch or powdered sugar, for dusting
⅓ pound (150 g) white fondant
½ cup (62 g) white Buttercream Frosting (see page ix)
Silver or gold mist food color spray
Rainbow disco dust (optional)

Equipment: 3¾-inch (9.5 cm) diamond ring cookie cutter, 1½-inch (3.75 cm) circle cookie cutter, parchment paper, piping bag, coupler, number 3 tip

1   Melt margarine over low heat in a 5-quart or larger saucepan. Add marshmallows, and stir. Let marshmallows melt completely, stirring occasionally. Remove from heat.

2   Stir in crisp rice cereal until covered with marshmallow. Turn out onto a greased baking sheet. With greased hands, press down into an even ½-inch (1.25 cm) thick layer. Cut out diamond ring shapes with ring cookie cutter. Using smaller circle cutter, cut out the inside of each ring band (you won't be using the smaller circles for the rings). Set diamond ring treats aside.

3   In preparation for working with fondant, dust a smooth, clean work surface with cornstarch or powdered sugar (to prevent sticking). Knead fondant by hand and roll out to about ⅛ inch (3 mm) thick. Cut out same size diamond ring shape from fondant. Spread a small amount of buttercream frosting on treat, then gently transfer cut fondant to treat.

4   Use a sheet of parchment paper to cover diamond part of ring and spray band with color mist spray. Outline and add details to diamond using buttercream frosting in a piping bag with a number 3 tip. For extra shimmer, sprinkle rainbow disco dust over diamond.

Wedding Monogram Treats

Crispy treats aren't just for kids anymore. These personalized treats would be a great addition to the dessert table at a wedding.

YIELD: 9 TO 12 TREATS
TIME: 2+ HOURS
DIFFICULTY LEVEL: ADVANCED

3 tbsp margarine
1 10-ounce (280 g) bag mini marshmallows
Gel food coloring of choice (optional)
6 cups (150 g) crisp rice cereal
1½ cups (187 g) Buttercream Frosting (see page ix)

Equipment: Parchment paper, 3-inch square cookie cutter, piping bag, coupler, number 3 tip

1 Before you begin, find a font you would like to use for the monogram. Print out monogram letters in the size you will need for treats on a piece of paper several times. Slip printed letters under a sheet of parchment paper and practice piping monogram until you are happy with results.

2 Melt margarine over low heat in a 5-quart or larger saucepan. Add marshmallows, and stir. Let marshmallows melt completely, stirring occasionally. Remove from heat. If you wish to make colored treats, add a few drops of gel food coloring and stir to combine. Continue adding gel coloring until desired shade is reached.

3 Stir in crisp rice cereal until covered with marshmallow. Turn out onto a greased baking sheet. With greased hands, press down into an even ½-inch (1.25 cm) thick layer. Cut out squares with cookie cutter.

4 Using buttercream frosting in a piping bag with a number 3 tip, pipe monogram onto each treat. The bottom side of treats will be the smoothest and flattest surface, so I suggest turning them over and piping on the bottom. Pipe the outline of the treat with buttercream frosting as well.

Treat Tip:

Piping the monogram directly onto the crispy treats can be difficult. If you think you might have trouble, spread a layer of buttercream frosting over the treat.

Chapter Four

Crispy Shapes

Ice Cream Cone Treats

Friends and family are bound to do a double-take when they see these amazing "ice cream" cones, which look so much like the real thing. A bonus of the crispy version: it won't melt on you!

YIELD: APPROXIMATELY 32 TREATS
TIME: 1½ HOURS ACTIVE,
20 MINUTES DRYING TIME
DIFFICULTY LEVEL: INTERMEDIATE

3 tbsp margarine
1 10-ounce (280 g) bag mini marshmallows
6 cups (150 g) crisp rice cereal
8 ounces (225 g) almond bark or candy melts
Sprinkles
2 cups (290 g) candy-coated chocolate balls
32 mini ice cream cones

Equipment: Cookie scoop

1 Melt margarine over low heat in a 5-quart or larger saucepan. Add marshmallows, and stir. Let marshmallows melt completely, stirring occasionally. Remove from heat.

2 Stir in crisp rice cereal until covered with marshmallow. As soon as mixture is cool enough to handle, begin making the "ice cream" scoops. Spray a cookie scoop with nonstick cooking spray. Pack scoop tightly with rice cereal mixture, leaving an uneven edge around the outside of the crispy treat scoop to make it look like real ice cream. Release onto a greased baking sheet. Repeat until all of cereal mixture has been used. Re-spray cookie scoop after every few uses; if scoop gets too sticky, wash with soap and water, dry, then spray with nonstick cooking spray again.

3 Using a microwave-safe dish, heat almond bark or candy melts in the microwave in 30-second increments until melted, stirring between each heating. (I recommend using High power level for first heating and switching to 50 percent power for subsequent heatings.) Drizzle over crispy scoop treats, and immediately add sprinkles and a candy-coated chocolate ball to each one.

4 Dip rim of a cone in almond bark. Next, fill cone with candy-coated chocolate balls (this will keep it from toppling over). Carefully place a crispy scoop on top of cone. Wait for almond bark to set completely. Repeat for rest of cones. Store in airtight container and serve within 24 hours.

Over-the-Cup Flowers with Fresh Fruit

• • • • • • • • • • • • •

These treats are perfect for a Mother's Day brunch or any occasion when you want to serve a light dessert with a bit of flair.

YIELD: APPROXIMATELY 30 FLOWERS
TIME: 1 HOUR
DIFFICULTY LEVEL: INTERMEDIATE

3 tbsp margarine
1 10-ounce (280 g) bag mini marshmallows
4 ounces (115 g) almond bark
6 to 7 cups (150–175 g) crisp rice cereal
1 cup (125 g) Buttercream Frosting (see page ix), tinted in color of choice
30 jumbo quins or other round candies
Fresh-cut fruit such as strawberries, blueberries, raspberries, pineapple

Equipment: 2½-inch (6 cm) flower-shape cookie cutter, piping bag, coupler, number 3 tip, small clear plastic cups or footed dessert bowls for serving

1 Melt margarine in a 5-quart or larger saucepan over low heat. Add marshmallows, and stir. Let marshmallows melt completely, stirring occasionally. Stir in almond bark until melted. Remove from heat.

2 Pour in 6 cups (150 g) of the rice cereal and stir until covered with marshmallow. If mixture looks too gooey, add 1 more cup (25 g) rice cereal. Turn out onto a greased baking sheet. With greased hands, press mixture down into a layer that is ½-inch (1.25 cm) thick. Let cool completely.

3 Cut out flower shapes using cookie cutter. With a sharp knife, cut a thin notch about halfway into each flower. (This notch will allow the flowers to rest on the rim of the serving cups/bowls.)

4 Using buttercream frosting, piping bag, and number 3 tip, pipe an outline around each flower. Attach 1 jumbo quin to center of each flower with buttercream frosting.

5 Just before serving, assemble fruit cups by placing some fresh fruit in each cup and hanging a flower treat on the rim. Make and serve treats on same day.

Barnyard Treats

These barn-shaped treats would be the perfect addition to any Western-themed event.

YIELD: APPROXIMATELY 12 BARNS
TIME: 45 MINUTES
DIFFICULTY LEVEL: EASY

3 tbsp margarine
1 10-ounce (280 g) bag
  mini marshmallows
Red gel food coloring
6 cups (150 g) crisp rice cereal
1 cup (125 g) white
  Buttercream Frosting
12 pig or cow gummies

Equipment: 3-inch (7.5 cm) barn cookie cutter, piping bag, coupler, number 3 tip

1 Melt margarine over low heat in a 5-quart or larger saucepan. Add marshmallows, and stir. Let marshmallows melt completely, stirring occasionally. Remove from heat. Add a few drops of red gel food coloring and stir to combine. Continue adding food coloring, a few drops at a time, until desired shade has been reached.

2 Stir in crisp rice cereal until covered with marshmallow. Turn out onto a greased baking sheet. With greased hands, press down into an even layer ½-inch (1.25 cm) thick. Use cookie cutter to cut out barns from crispy mixture.

3 Outline barn and door with buttercream frosting, using a piping bag and number 3 tip. Affix gummy animal to treat with a small pile of frosting. Press down onto gummy firmly and allow frosting to set.

4 Store in an airtight container in the refrigerator and serve within 24 hours.

Awareness Ribbon Treats

• • • • • • • • • • • • •

Show your support by making these awareness ribbon treats in the color of a cause that is important to you.

YIELD: APPROXIMATELY 12
AWARENESS RIBBONS
TIME: 45 MINUTES
DIFFICULTY LEVEL: EASY

3 tbsp margarine

1 10-ounce (280 g) bag
    mini marshmallows

Gel food coloring in color
    of cause

6 cups (150 g) crisp rice cereal

1½ cups (187 g) Buttercream
    Frosting (see page ix),
    tinted color of cause

Sanding sugar, color of
    cause (optional)

Equipment: 4-inch (10 cm)
long ribbon cookie cutter,
piping bag (optional), coupler
(optional), number 3 tip
(optional)

1   Melt margarine over low heat in a 5-quart or larger saucepan. Add marshmallows, and stir. Let marshmallows melt completely, stirring occasionally. Remove from heat. Add a few drops of gel food coloring and stir to incorporate. Continue adding gel coloring until desired shade is reached.

2   Stir in crisp rice cereal until covered with marshmallow. Turn out onto a greased baking sheet. With greased hands, press down into an even layer ½-inch (1.25 cm) thick. Cut out ribbon shapes using cookie cutter.

3   To decorate, either outline ribbon with buttercream frosting using a piping bag and number 3 tip or cover entire ribbon in frosting and dip in matching-colored sanding sugar.

4   Store treats in an airtight container in the refrigerator and serve within 24 hours.

Donut Treats

When guests first lay their eyes on these treats, they'll find it hard to believe that they aren't actual donuts. The delicious buttercream frosting and sprinkles go a long way toward pulling off the disguise.

YIELD: 12 DONUTS
TIME: 30 MINUTES ACTIVE,
20 MINUTES COOLING
DIFFICULTY LEVEL: EASY

3 tbsp margarine
1 10-ounce (280 g) bag
   mini marshmallows
6 cups (150 g) crisp rice cereal
1½ cups (187 g) Buttercream
   Frosting (see page ix),
   tinted color(s) of choice
Sprinkles

Equipment: Donut baking pan

1 Melt margarine over low heat in a 5-quart or larger saucepan. Add marshmallows, and stir. Let marshmallows melt completely, stirring occasionally. Remove from heat.

2 Stir in crisp rice cereal until covered with marshmallow. As soon as mixture is cool enough to handle, press into a greased donut baking pan to form donut-shaped treats. (If necessary, turn out formed treats onto a greased baking sheet and reuse donut pan until all of the mixture has been used.) Let cool completely.

3 Frost donuts with buttercream frosting and top with sprinkles. Store in an airtight container in the refrigerator and serve within 24 hours.

Treat Tip:
For something different, try using the Maple Frosting from the Candied Bacon and Maple Treats on page 96.

Fishbowl Treats

· · · · · · · · · · · · · · · ·

Decorating these charming treats is a wonderful activity for kids.

YIELD: 9 TREATS
TIME: 1½ HOURS
DIFFICULTY LEVEL: INTERMEDIATE

3 tbsp margarine

1 10-ounce (280 g) bag mini marshmallows

6 cups (150 g) crisp rice cereal

¾ cup (94 g) Buttercream Frosting (see page ix), tinted blue

½ cup turbinado sugar

Fish candies

White pearl nonpareils

¾ cup (TK g) Buttercream Frosting, tinted green

Equipment: 3½-inch (8.75 cm) circle cookie cutter, piping bag, coupler, number 2 tip

1 Melt margarine over low heat in a 5-quart or larger saucepan. Add marshmallows, and stir. Let marshmallows melt completely, stirring occasionally. Remove from heat.

2 Stir in crisp rice cereal until covered with marshmallow. Turn out onto a greased baking sheet. With greased hands, press down into an even ½-inch (1.25 cm) thick layer. Cut out circles with cookie cutter. Gently press top of each circle flat to form the shape of a fishbowl.

3 Create the "water" for the fishbowl with blue buttercream frosting. It helps to pipe an outline for the water first (create a wave design toward the top) and then spread the frosting on with a knife. For "sand," add turbinado sugar toward bottom of fishbowl. Arrange goldfish candies on top of blue frosting, and add white pearl nonpareils (for bubbles) near the mouth of each. Pipe on some aquarium plants with green frosting, using a piping bag and a number 2 tip.

Variation:
To create a funky aquarium, use sanding sugar in bright colors instead of the turbinado sugar.

Turtle Treats

Making these treats is another great project to do with kids on a rainy afternoon or as a party activity. The decorating scheme I've outlined below is merely one possible approach. There are all sorts of ways to make these turtles fun and adorable.

YIELD: 8 TURTLES
TIME: 1 HOUR
DIFFICULTY LEVEL: EASY

3 tbsp margarine
1 10-ounce (280 g) bag mini marshmallows
Leaf-green gel food coloring
6 cups (150 g) crisp rice cereal
Black candy writer
8 candy eyes
1 cup (125 g) Buttercream Frosting (see page ix), tinted green
8 to 9 feet (2.5–2.75 m) green licorice string
⅙ pound (75 g) candy-coated chocolates in dark green
⅙ pound (75 g) candy-coated chocolates in light green

Equipment: 1½ x 5-inch (3.75 x 12.75 cm) turtle cookie cutter

1 Melt margarine over low heat in a 5-quart or larger saucepan. Add marshmallows, and stir. Let marshmallows melt completely, stirring occasionally. Remove from heat. Add a few drops of green gel coloring and stir to incorporate. Continue adding gel coloring until desired shade is reached.

2 Stir in crisp rice cereal until covered with marshmallow. Turn out onto a greased baking sheet. With greased hands, press down into an even ½-inch (1.25 cm) thick layer. Cut out turtle shapes with cookie cutter.

3 Draw a mouth on each turtle with black candy writer. Use a small dot from candy writer to glue on a candy eye. Frost turtle shells with green buttercream frosting, and outline them with green licorice string. Next, cover shells with candy-coated chocolates, alternating shades of green.

4 Store in an airtight container in the refrigerator and serve within 24 hours.

Tip Treat:
I usually buy a big bag of M&M's and use the green ones to decorate this treat, but feel free to be creative with your turtle decorations!

Flip-Flop Treats

. . . .

Inject a bit of whimsy into your next picnic or pool party with these adorable flip-flop treats.

YIELD: 9 FLIP-FLOPS
TIME: 1 HOUR
DIFFICULTY: EASY TO
INTERMEDIATE

3 tbsp margarine
1 10-ounce (280 g) bag
   mini marshmallows
Gel food coloring of choice
   (optional)
6 cups (150 g) crisp rice cereal
5 feet (1.5 m) licorice string

Equipment: 4-inch
(10 cm) long egg-shaped
cookie cutter, paring knife,
toothpick, piping bag
(optional), coupler (optional),
number 2 or 3 tip (optional)

1   Melt margarine over low heat in a 5-quart or larger saucepan. Add marshmallows, and stir. Let marshmallows melt completely, stirring occasionally. Remove from heat. For colored crispy treats, add a few drops of gel food coloring and stir to combine. Continue adding gel coloring until desired shade is reached.

2   Stir in crisp rice cereal until covered with marshmallow. Turn out onto a greased baking sheet. With greased hands, press down into an even ½-inch (1.25 cm) thick layer. Cut out egg shapes with cookie cutter. Gently press sides of egg inward to mold into shoe shape. The narrowest part of the egg should be the heel of the flip-flop.

3   Use a paring knife to cut a small slit in middle of toe area of flip-flop. Cut licorice string about 6 inches (15 cm) long. Fold licorice in half and twist the midpoint (where the bend is) one full time around. Insert midpoint into toe slit of flip-flop. Gently push cereal mixture back around licorice to secure. With a toothpick, poke two holes on each side of top of shoe for other ends of licorice straps. Push licorice ends through the holes and push cereal mixture back together to secure.

4   Store treats in an airtight container (in the refrigerator if they include frosting) and serve within 24 hours.

Butterfly Crispy Treats

These butterfly treats provide the perfect canvas for letting your creative juices flow. From the colors you choose to the edible embellishments you select, the possibilities are endless.

YIELD: APPROXIMATELY 9 BUTTERFLIES
TIME: 1 HOUR
DIFFICULTY: EASY

3 tbsp margarine
1 10-ounce (280 g) bag mini marshmallows
Gel food coloring of choice (optional)
6 cups (150 g) crisp rice cereal
9 sour straws
1½ cups (187 g) Buttercream Frosting (see page ix), tinted color of choice
Quins, sprinkles, assorted candies

Equipment: 4-inch (10 cm) wide butterfly cookie cutter, piping bag, coupler, number 3 tip

1 Melt margarine over low heat in a 5-quart or larger saucepan. Add marshmallows, and stir. Let marshmallows melt completely, stirring occasionally. Remove from heat. For colored crispy treats, add a few drops of gel food coloring and stir to combine. Continue adding gel coloring until desired shade is reached.

2 Stir in crisp rice cereal until covered with marshmallow. Turn out onto a greased baking sheet. With greased hands, press down into an even ½-inch (1.25 cm) thick layer. Cut out butterfly shapes with cookie cutter.

3 Cut sour straws to the length of butterfly body plus 1 inch (2.5 cm). With a sharp knife, split one end of each sour straw in half about 1 inch (2.5 cm) down to form antennae. Using a piping bag and number 3 tip, pipe a thin line of buttercream frosting down center of butterfly and attach sour straw. Decorate wings with frosting, sprinkles, quins, and/or candy. Repeat for rest of treats.

4 Store in an airtight container in the refrigerator and serve within 24 hours.

Dinosaur Diorama Treats

• • • • • • • • • • • • •

You can make this dessert ahead of time by storing the chocolate base and dinosaurs separately in an airtight container for up to 24 hours.

YIELD: APPROXIMATELY 24
2-INCH (5 CM) SQUARE SERVINGS
TIME: 1½ HOURS
DIFFICULTY LEVEL: ADVANCED

Diorama Base

3 tbsp margarine
1 10-ounce (280 g) bag mini marshmallows
6 cups (150 g) chocolate crisp rice cereal
Candy jelly rocks

Dinosaurs

2 tbsp margarine
2¾ cups (5 ounces [140 g]) mini marshmallows
¼ cup green candy melts (56 g) or 4 ounces (115 g) white almond bark
Green gel food coloring
3 cups (75 g) crisp rice cereal
1 cup (125 g) Buttercream Frosting (see page ix)

Equipment: 9 x 13-inch (22 x 33 cm) baking dish, 8 x 8-inch (20 x 20 cm) baking dish, dinosaur cookie cutters, tree and bush cake picks

1 First make the diorama base. Melt margarine over low heat in a 5-quart or larger saucepan. Add marshmallows, and stir. Let marshmallows melt completely, stirring occasionally. Remove from heat. Stir in chocolate cereal until covered with marshmallow. Turn out into 9 × 13-inch (22 × 33 cm) baking dish and press into an even layer. Set aside to cool.

2 Next make the dinosaurs. Melt margarine over low heat in a 3-quart or larger saucepan. Add marshmallows, and stir. Let marshmallows melt completely, stirring occasionally. Add in green candy melts and stir until completely melted. Remove from heat. Add a few drops of green gel food coloring and mix to incorporate. Continue to add gel coloring until desired shade is reached.

3 Stir in crisp rice cereal. Turn out into an 8 × 8-inch (20 × 20 cm) baking dish and press into an even layer. Immediately cut two dinosaurs from green treat mixture.

4 Decorate dinosaurs with buttercream frosting. Add eyes, mouth, and any other details.

5 Shortly before serving, assemble the diorama: Place dinosaurs on top of the chocolate crispy layer. (If desired for an added wow factor, turn out onto cake board first.) The dinosaurs should stick to the chocolate crispy base, but if you're having trouble getting them to stay put, add some frosting to keep them in place. Add tree and bush cake picks and candy jelly rocks to complete the scene.

Puppy Paw Treats

These puppy paws are easy to make but have a big visual impact. Pet lovers young and old will love these chocolate-flavored treats.

YIELD: 16 TO 20 PAWS
TIME: 30 MINUTES
DIFFICULTY LEVEL: EASY

3 tbsp margarine
1 10-ounce (280 g) bag
  mini marshmallows
6 cups (150 g) chocolate
  crisp rice cereal
20 white or light brown
  candy melts (or 10 of each)
¼ cup white chocolate chips
  or peanut butter chips
  (or a mix of both)

Equipment: 2½-inch (6 cm)
paw print cookie cutter

1 Melt margarine over low heat in a 5-quart or larger saucepan. Add marshmallows, and stir. Let marshmallows melt completely, stirring occasionally. Remove from heat.

2 Stir in chocolate crisp rice cereal until covered with marshmallow. Turn out onto a greased baking sheet and press into an even ½-inch (1.25 cm) thick layer. Cut out paws with cookie cutter.

3 Press a candy melt into center of each paw. Press four small chips, tip side down, into toes of paws.

4 Store in an airtight container on countertop and serve within 24 hours.

Clam Shell Treats

· · · • · • · • • · • • · • · •

Every little mermaid will love these seashells, complete with a pearl gumball inside.

YIELD: 8 CLAM SHELLS
TIME: 45 MINUTES
DIFFICULTY LEVEL: EASY

3 tbsp margarine
1 10-ounce (280 g) bag
   mini marshmallows
Pink gel food coloring
6 cups (150 g) crisp rice cereal
8 shimmer white or pink
   gumballs
1.5 cups (187 g) white
   Buttercream Frosting
   (see page ix)

Equipment: 3-inch (7.5 cm)
shell cookie cutter, piping
bag, coupler, number 3 tip

1 Melt margarine over low heat in a 5-quart or larger saucepan. Add marshmallows, and stir. Let marshmallows melt completely, stirring occasionally. Remove from heat. Add a few drops of pink gel food coloring and stir to combine. Continue adding gel coloring until desired shade is reached.

2 Stir in crisp rice cereal until covered with marshmallow. Turn out onto a greased baking sheet. With greased hands, press down into an even layer ½-inch (1.25 cm) thick. Cut out shell shapes with cookie cutter.

3 Place a gumball on top of one shell. Take a second shell and line it up with bottom shell. Press small ends of the shells together. Outline top shell with buttercream frosting using a piping bag and a number 3 tip. Repeat for rest of treats.

4 Store in an airtight container in the refrigerator and serve within 24 hours.

Chocolate-Covered Strawberry Treats

• • • • • • • • • • • • •

Everyone loves chocolate-covered strawberries. Dazzle your guests by creating crispy treats that mimic the real thing.

YIELD: 24 TO 30
STRAWBERRY TREATS
TIME: 1½ HOURS
DIFFICULTY LEVEL: ADVANCED

3 tbsp margarine
1 10-ounce (280 g) bag
   mini marshmallows
¼ cup (28 g) powdered
   strawberry gelatin
6 cups (150 g) crisp rice cereal
1 pound (455 g) dipping
   chocolate
4 ounces (115 g) white
   dipping chocolate
Powdered sugar, for dusting
8 ounces (225 g) green
   fondant or green taffy

Equipment: Parchment
paper, piping bag, small
flower cookie cutter

1 Melt margarine over low heat in a 5-quart or larger saucepan. Add marshmallows, and stir. Let marshmallows melt completely, stirring occasionally. Add powdered strawberry gelatin and stir until completely combined. Remove from heat.

2 Pour in crisp rice cereal and stir until covered with marshmallow. Coat clean hands with nonstick cooking spray, butter, or margarine. While mixture is still warm, form it into 24 to 30 strawberry shapes with your hands. Place strawberry treats on a piece of parchment paper or a baking sheet that has been sprayed with nonstick cooking spray. If mixture becomes difficult to work with, place unformed cereal mixture on stove top over low heat until pliable again. Coat your hands with nonstick cooking spray as many times as necessary to prevent mixture from sticking to them. Let cool.

3 Once strawberry treats are cool, it's time to dip them in chocolate. Using a microwave-safe bowl, heat dipping chocolate in the microwave on 50 percent power in 30-second increments, until completely melted. Stir between each heating. Dip each strawberry treat in chocolate, gently shake off any excess, and place on a sheet of parchment paper. Repeat until all strawberries have been dipped. If dipping chocolate becomes thick

and difficult to work with, reheat for 30 seconds at 50 percent power. Place strawberries aside until chocolate has completely set.

4 Melt a small amount of white dipping chocolate according to directions in step 3. Put melted white chocolate in a pastry bag or small plastic baggie. Cut a small piece off tip of bag and drizzle white chocolate over strawberry treats.

5 While white chocolate is setting, create leafy green strawberry tops. Dust the surface on which you'll be cutting fondant with powdered sugar (to prevent sticking). Work green taffy or fondant in your hands to make it malleable. Using a knife, cut a leafy stem for each strawberry treat out of fondant and attach to treats. (If fondant is sticking to knife, coat knife with a little nonstick cooking spray.) The treats will be sticky at the top, so no additional steps are necessary for fondant to adhere. Store in an airtight container on countertop. Best if served the same day.

Chapter Five

Crispy Treats Squared

Candied Bacon and Maple Treats

The salty and smoky bacon flavor complements the sweet maple frosting for an amazing taste. Make and store in an airtight container up to 24 hours in advance!

YIELD: 24 2-INCH (5 CM) SQUARES
TIME: 1½ HOURS ACTIVE.
20 MINUTES COOKING TIME
DIFFICULTY LEVEL: ADVANCED

Candied Bacon
¾ cup (170 g) brown sugar
1 tsp ground cinnamon
1 pound (455 g) bacon

Maple Frosting
¼ cup (55 g) butter, room
    temperature
1 tsp vanilla extract
⅓ cup (60 ml) pure maple syrup
½ tsp salt
2 to 3 cups (200–300 g)
    powdered sugar
1 tsp milk, if needed

Rice Cereal Mixture
3 tbsp margarine
1 10-ounce (280 g) bag mini
    marshmallows
1 tsp maple extract
6 cups (150 g) crisp rice cereal

Equipment: 9 x 13-inch
(22 x 33 cm) baking dish

1 Preheat oven to 350°F (180°C). To make the candied bacon, mix brown sugar and cinnamon in a bowl and press bacon slices into the mixture, coating both sides.

2 Place coated bacon slices on an oven-safe cooling rack set on top of a baking sheet. Bake for approximately 15 to 20 minutes or until bacon is crispy. Let cool. Chop into bacon-bit-size pieces, and set aside.

3 Next make the maple frosting. Cream together butter, vanilla, maple syrup, salt, and 1 cup (100 g) of the powdered sugar. Once completely combined, add more sugar, 1 cup (100 g) at a time, until desired thickness is reached. If frosting becomes too thick, thin with a teaspoon of milk. Store covered in refrigerator until ready to use.

4 Finally, make the rice cereal mixture. Melt margarine over low heat in a 5-quart or larger saucepan. Add marshmallows, and stir. Let marshmallows melt completely, stirring occasionally. Add maple extract and stir to combine. Remove from heat.

5 Pour in crisp rice cereal and stir until covered with marshmallow. Fold ½ cup (40 g) of the candied bacon into rice cereal mixture. Spread mixture your baking dish that has been well coated with nonstick cooking spray. Push down evenly and let cool.

6 Right before serving, spread maple frosting over treat mixture (be sure to remove frosting from the refrigerator about 20 to 30 minutes in advance so it's softened). Sprinkle with remaining candied bacon bits.

Cranberry Orange Crispy Treats

Cranberry and orange are a classic holiday duo. Orange juice and zest give these treats a bright flavor that pairs splendidly with the sweet and tart cranberries. Surprise your neighbors with some of these treats during the holiday season.

YIELD: 24 2-INCH (5 CM) SQUARES
TIME: 40 MINUTES
DIFFICULTY LEVEL: EASY

3 tbsp margarine
1 10-ounce (280 g) bag mini marshmallows
Zest from 1 medium orange
2 tbsp orange juice
6 cups (150 g) crisp rice cereal
1 cup (120 g) roughly chopped dried cranberries

Equipment: 9 x 13-inch (22 x 33 cm) baking dish

1 Melt margarine over low heat in a 5-quart or larger saucepan. Add marshmallows, and stir. Let marshmallows melt completely, stirring occasionally. Add orange zest and juice, and stir to combine. Remove from heat.

2 Pour in rice cereal and dried cranberries, and stir until covered with marshmallow mixture. Spread mixture into a 9 × 13-inch (22 × 33 cm) baking dish that has been well coated with nonstick spray. Push down evenly with greased hands or spatula. Let cool.

3 Store in an airtight container on countertop and serve within 24 hours. Just before serving, cut into 2-inch (5 cm) squares.

Treat 411:
You'll find that the orange juice takes some of the stickiness away from the marshmallows, but don't worry. After the treat mixture has had time to set, everything will stick together.

Salted Caramel Crispy Treats

Salt has an almost magical way of enhancing something sweet, as it does in these salted caramel treats. I recommend splurging for some sea salt flakes; they really put this dessert over the top, giving it a gourmet look.

YIELD: 24 2-INCH (5 CM) SQUARES
TIME: 1 HOUR
DIFFICULTY LEVEL: EASY

4 tbsp butter
1 11-ounce (311 g) bag caramel bits
1 14-ounce (425 ml) can sweetened condensed milk
3 tbsp margarine
1 10-ounce (280 g) bag mini marshmallows
6 cups (150 g) crisp rice cereal
1 tbsp water
2 tsp sea salt flakes or coarse sea salt

Equipment: 9 x 13-inch (22 x 33 cm) baking dish

1 In a heavy saucepan, melt together butter, caramel bits, and sweetened condensed milk. Remove caramel sauce from heat and set aside.

2 Next, melt margarine in a 5-quart or larger saucepan. Add marshmallows, and stir. Let marshmallows melt completely, stirring occasionally. Add 1 cup of the caramel sauce and stir to combine, then remove from heat.

3 Pour in crisp rice cereal and stir until covered with marshmallow. Spread into a 9 × 13-inch (22 × 33 cm) baking dish that has been well coated with nonstick cooking spray. Push mixture down evenly with greased hands or spatula.

4 Place remaining caramel sauce over low heat and add 1 tablespoon of water to thin it to a spreading consistency. Pour over treat mixture and spread with knife so top is completely covered. Sprinkle sea salt flakes over the caramel before it has time to set. Let cool.

5 Store in an airtight container on countertop and serve within 24 hours. Shortly before serving, cut into 2-inch (5 cm) squares.

Double-Mint Chocolate Crispy Treats

· · · · · · · · · · · ·

The pairing of mint and chocolate is a beloved flavor combination that translates well to crispy treats.

YIELD: 24 2-INCH (5 CM) SQUARES
TIME: 1 HOUR
DIFFICULTY LEVEL: EASY

Rice Cereal Mixture

½ cup (70 g) crème de menthe baking chips
3 tbsp margarine
1 10-ounce (280 g) mini marshmallows
½ tsp mint extract
Green food coloring (optional)
6 cups (150 g) crisp rice cereal

Topping

2 cups (340 g) chocolate chips
1 cup (140 g) crème de menthe baking chips

Equipment: 9 x 13-inch (22 x 33 cm) baking dish

1 Place ½ cup (70 g) crème de menthe baking chips in freezer for at least 1 hour before preparing treats.

2 Melt margarine over low heat in a 5-quart or larger saucepan. Add marshmallows, and stir. Let marshmallows melt completely, stirring occasionally. Stir in mint extract and remove from heat. If desired, add a few drops of green food coloring and stir until completely combined.

3 Pour in rice cereal and stir. When melted marshmallow mixture and cereal are almost completely combined, add frozen crème de menthe baking chips and stir to incorporate. Turn out into a 9 × 13-inch (22 × 33 cm) baking dish that has been well coated with nonstick cooking spray. Push mixture down evenly with a greased hands or spatula. Let cool.

4 For the topping: In a 2- or 3-quart saucepan, melt chocolate chips and 1 cup (140 g) crème de menthe baking chips over medium-low heat, stirring constantly. When completely melted, pour over treat mixture and spread evenly. Let cool until mint-chocolate has set.

5 Store in an airtight container on countertop and serve within 24 hours. Cut into 2-inch (5 cm) squares just before serving.

White Chocolate Macadamia Nut Treats

One of my favorite types of cookie is white chocolate macadamia nut. Happily, the flavors translate well to rice crispy treats.

YIELD: 24 2-INCH (5 CM) SQUARES
TIME: 45 MINUTES
DIFFICULTY LEVEL: EASY

1 cup (175 g) white chocolate chips

3 tbsp margarine

1 10-ounce (280 g) bag mini marshmallows

6 cups (150 g) crisp rice cereal

1 cup (125 g) chopped macadamia nuts

4 ounces (115 g) almond bark or ½ cup (85 g) white chocolate chips

Equipment: 9 x 13-inch (22 x 33 cm) baking dish

1 Freeze white chocolate chips for at least 1 hour before making treats.

2 Melt margarine over low heat in a 5-quart or larger saucepan. Add marshmallows, and stir. Let marshmallows melt completely, stirring occasionally. Remove from heat.

3 Pour in crisp rice cereal and stir until covered with marshmallow. Fold in ⅔ cup (85 g) of the macadamia nuts, as well as the frozen white chocolate chips. Spread into a 9 × 13-inch (22 × 33 cm) baking dish that has been well coated with nonstick cooking spray. Push down evenly with greased hands or spatula.

4 Using a microwave-safe dish, heat almond bark in the microwave in 30-second increments until completely melted, stirring between each heating. (I recommend using High power level for first heating and switching to 50 percent power for subsequent heatings.) Drizzle melted almond bark over crispy treat mixture, and then quickly sprinkle remaining ⅓ cup (40 g) of macadamia nuts on top. Let cool.

5 Store in an airtight container on countertop and serve within 24 hours. Just before serving, cut into 2-inch (5 cm) squares.

Orange Cream Crispy Treats

• • • , • • • • • • • • • • •

My favorite ice cream growing up was an orange Creamsicle. These treats take me right back to my childhood. While it's not necessary, you'll achieve a more dramatic visual contrast by making the vanilla layer white here.

YIELD: 24 2-INCH (5 CM) SQUARES
TIME: 1 HOUR
DIFFICULTY LEVEL: EASY

Orange Treat Mixture

3 tbsp margarine
1 10-ounce (280 g) bag mini marshmallows
2 tsp orange extract
Orange food coloring
6 cups (150 g) crisp rice cereal

Vanilla Treat Mixture

2 tbsp margarine
2¾ cups (5 ounces [140 g]) mini marshmallows
1 tsp clear vanilla extract
Bright white gel food coloring (optional)
3 cups (75 g) crisp rice cereal

Equipment: 9 x 13-inch (22 x 33 cm) baking dish

1 For the orange treat mixture, melt margarine over low heat in a 5-quart or larger saucepan. Add marshmallows, and stir. Let marshmallows melt completely, stirring occasionally. Stir in orange extract and remove from heat. Add a few drops of orange food coloring and stir to combine. Continue adding food coloring, a few drops at a time, until desired shade is attained. Pour in rice cereal and stir until covered with marshmallow.

2 At the same time, make the vanilla treat mixture. Melt margarine in a second saucepan. Add marshmallows and stir occasionally until completely melted. Stir in vanilla extract and remove from heat. If desired, add a few drops of white gel food coloring. Pour in rice cereal and stir until covered with marshmallow. Set aside.

3 Turn out half of the orange treat mixture into a greased 9 × 13-inch (22 × 33 cm) baking dish. Press down evenly and firmly. Add vanilla treat mixture on top and press out into an even layer. Place the second half of the orange mixture on top and press into an even layer. Let cool completely.

4 Store in an airtight container and serve within 24 hours. Shortly before serving, cut into 2-inch (5 cm) squares.

Peppermint White Chocolate Crispy Treats

• • • • • • • • • • • • •

Don't let the stress of holiday baking get you down. Serve these no-bake crispy treats, instead. Delicious, pretty, and easy to make, they're sure to be a hit at any festive gathering.

YIELD: 24 2-INCH (5 CM) SQUARES
TIME: 30 MINUTES
DIFFICULTY LEVEL: EASY

3 tbsp margarine

1 10-ounce (280 g) bag mini marshmallows

1 cup (175 g) white chocolate chips

1 tsp peppermint extract

6 cups (150 g) crisp rice cereal

¾ cup (180 g) peppermint baking pieces or crushed candy cane

2 ounces (55 g) almond bark or white chocolate

Equipment: 9 x 13-inch (22 x 33 cm) baking dish

1 Melt margarine over low heat in a 5-quart or larger saucepan. Add marshmallows, and stir. Let marshmallows melt completely, stirring occasionally. Stir in white chocolate chips and peppermint extract until chips are completely incorporated. Remove from heat.

2 Pour in rice cereal and stir until covered with marshmallow. Fold in ½ cup (120 g) of the peppermint pieces. Turn out mixture into a 9 × 13-inch (22 × 33 cm) baking dish that has been well coated with nonstick cooking spray. Push mixture down evenly with greased hands or spatula.

3 Using a microwave-safe dish, heat almond bark in the microwave in 30-second increments until completely melted, stirring between each heating. (I recommend using High power level for first heating and switching to 50 percent power for subsequent heatings.) Drizzle over treat mixture. Next, sprinkle remaining ¼ cup (60 g) peppermint pieces over treat mixture.

4 Store in an airtight container on countertop and serve within 24 hours. Cut into 2-inch (5 cm squares) shortly before serving.

Cookie Butter Treats

Cookie butter is a lot like peanut butter, but it's made from blended cookies instead of nuts. There are a few different brands of cookie butter, so you should be able to find some at your local grocery store or fine food retailer.

YIELD: 24 2-INCH (5 CM) SQUARES
TIME: 20 MINUTES
DIFFICULTY LEVEL: EASY

3 tbsp margarine
1 10-ounce (280 g) bag mini marshmallows
½ cup (130 g) cookie butter
6 cups (180 g) crisp rice cereal

Equipment: 9 x 13-inch (22 x 33 cm) baking dish

1 Melt margarine over low heat in a 5-quart or larger saucepan. Add marshmallows, and stir. Let marshmallows melt completely, stirring occasionally. Add cookie butter and stir to combine. Remove from heat.

2 Pour in rice cereal and stir until covered with marshmallow mixture. Turn out into a 9 × 13-inch (22 × 33 cm) baking dish that has been well coated with nonstick cooking spray. Push mixture down evenly with greased hands or spatula. Let cool.

3 Store in an airtight container and serve within 24 hours. Shortly before serving, cut into 2-inch (5 cm) squares.

Treat 411:
The cookie butter will thicken up the marshmallows quite a bit. It might take a bit of an arm workout, but don't give up! These ingredients will mix together completely.

Toasted Coconut Crispy Treats

Why buy toasted coconut marshmallows when you can make your own version with crispy treats? This recipe is naturally dairy-free, with coconut oil standing in for butter or margarine.

YIELD: 24 2-INCH (5 CM) SQUARES
TIME: 1¼ HOURS
DIFFICULTY LEVEL: INTERMEDIATE

Coconut Marshmallows

1 cup (70 g) sweetened shredded coconut
1½ cups (75 g) mini marshmallows

Rice Cereal Mixture

3 tbsp coconut oil
1 10-ounce (280 g) bag mini marshmallows
6 cups (150 g) crisp rice cereal

Equipment: 9 x 13-inch (22 x 33 cm) baking dish

1 Place coconut in a sauté pan over medium heat, and stir frequently until toasted to a golden brown color. Remove from heat.

2 Pulse toasted coconut in a food processor to break it into fine pieces. Set aside.

3 Place 1½ cups (75 g) marshmallows in a freezer-safe rectangular plastic storage container with a lid. Using a spray bottle, lightly mist the marshmallows with water. Sprinkle the toasted coconut over the marshmallows, place the lid on the container and shake to coat marshmallows with coconut. (The water makes the marshmallows sticky.) Place in freezer.

4 Heat coconut oil over low heat in a 5-quart or larger saucepan. Add 10 ounces (280 g) mini marshmallows and heat until completely melted, stirring occasionally. Remove from heat.

5 Pour in rice cereal and stir until covered with marshmallow. Set aside for 5 minutes. Fold in coconut marshmallows, plus any toasted coconut left in container. The coconut-coated marshmallows should not melt completely.

6 Turn out mixture into your baking dish that has been well coated with nonstick cooking spray. Push down evenly, and let cool completely.

7 Store in an airtight container on countertop and serve within 24 hours. Just before serving, cut into 2-inch (5 cm) squares.

Dark Chocolate Raspberry Treats

• • • • • • • • • • • • •

Dark chocolate and raspberry is the perfect combination for the sophisticated palate—or any chocoholic. A double dose of chocolate imbues these treats with decadence, while the fresh raspberry elevates them to sublime.

YIELD: 24 2-INCH (5 CM) SQUARES
TIME: 1 HOUR
DIFFICULTY LEVEL: EASY

Raspberry Sauce

12 ounces (340 g) raspberries
½ cup (100 g) sugar
1 tsp lemon juice

Rice Cereal Mixture

3 tbsp margarine
1 10-ounce (280 g) bag mini marshmallows
½ cup (85 g) dark chocolate chips
1 tsp raspberry extract
6 cups (150 g) chocolate crisp rice cereal

Equipment: 9 x 13-inch (22 x 33 cm) baking dish

1 In a small saucepan, heat raspberries, sugar, and lemon juice over medium heat. Bring to a boil and let simmer for 3 minutes, stirring occasionally.

2 Blend raspberry sauce until smooth. Pour through a fine strainer to remove seeds. Refrigerate until ready to use.

3 Melt margarine in a 5-quart or larger saucepan over low heat. Add marshmallows and stir occasionally, until completely melted. Mix in dark chocolate chips and raspberry extract. Stir until chocolate chips are completely melted. Remove from heat.

4 Pour in chocolate rice cereal and stir until covered with marshmallow. Turn out into a 9 × 13-inch (22 × 33 cm) baking dish that has been well coated with nonstick cooking spray. Push mixture down with greased hands or spatula. Let cool.

5 Store in an airtight container on countertop, and enjoy within 24 hours. Just before serving, drizzle on the cold raspberry sauce and cut into 2-inch (5 cm) squares.

Triple-Crunch Peanut Butter Chocolate Treats

Crisp rice cereal, chunky peanut butter, and chopped nuts give these treats a whole lot of crunch. Unlike almost all of the other recipes in the book, this one is marshmallow free.

YIELD: 24 2-INCH (5 CM) SQUARES
TIME: 45 MINUTES
DIFFICULTY LEVEL: EASY

1 cup (235 ml) corn syrup
1 cup (200 g) sugar
1 cup (260 g) chunky peanut butter
6 cups (150 g) crisp rice cereal
1 cup (175 g) chocolate chips
1 cup (175 g) peanut butter chips
¼ cup (30 g) chopped nut topping

Equipment: 9 x 13-inch (22 x 33 cm) baking dish

1 Heat corn syrup and sugar over medium heat until sugar is dissolved and mixture begins to boil. Remove from heat and stir in chunky peanut butter.

2 Pour in crisp rice cereal and stir to coat. Turn out into greased 9 × 13-inch (22 × 33 cm) baking dish. Set aside.

3 In a small saucepan, melt chocolate chips and peanut butter chips over medium-low heat. Stir occasionally until completely melted. Spread over rice cereal mixture. Sprinkle with nut topping. Let stand until chocolate has set

4 Store in an airtight container on countertop and serve within 24 hours. Just before serving, cut into 2-inch (5 cm) bars.

Variation:
If you'd prefer not to use corn syrup, you can try a substitution of 1 cup (340 g) of honey. Honey can also burn more easily, so watch your temperatures.

Chunky Monkey Crispy Treats

Inspired by the popular ice cream flavor, these chunky monkey treats can be enjoyed without risk of brain freeze!

YIELDS: 24 2-INCH (5 CM) SQUARES
TIME: 1 HOUR
DIFFICULTY LEVEL: EASY

1 cup (175 g) chocolate chips

3 tbsp margarine

1 10-ounce (280 g) bag
  mini marshmallows

1 3.4-ounce (96 g) package
  banana instant pudding mix

6 cups (150 g) crisp rice cereal

1 cup (125 g) chopped walnuts

Equipment: 9 x 13-inch
(22 x 33 cm) baking dish

1 Freeze chocolate chips for at least 1 hour before making treats.

2 Melt margarine over low heat in a 5-quart or larger saucepan. Add marshmallows, and stir. Let marshmallows melt completely, stirring occasionally. Add banana pudding mix and stir to combine. Remove from heat.

3 Pour in rice cereal and stir until covered with marshmallow mixture. Fold in chopped walnuts and frozen chocolate chips. Spread rice cereal mixture into a 9 × 13-inch (22 × 33 cm) baking dish that has been well coated with nonstick cooking spray. Push down evenly with greased hands or spatula. Let cool.

4 Store in an airtight container and serve within 24 hours. Cut into 2-inch (5 cm) squares just before serving.

Did You Know?
Freezing the chocolate chips allows them to hold their shape when added to the warm crispy treat mixture.

Peaches and Cream Crispy Treats

These peach-flavored crispy treats are finished off with a dollop of whipped topping, making for a sweet dessert that tastes like summer.

YIELD: 24 2-INCH (5 CM) SQUARES
TIME: 1¼ HOURS
DIFFICULTY LEVEL: EASY

3 tbsp margarine

1 10-ounce (280 g) bag mini marshmallows

1 3-ounce (85 g) box peach gelatin powder

6 cups (180 g) crisp rice cereal

¾ cup (150 g) chopped dried peaches (optional)

1 8-ounce (225 g) tub whipped topping

Equipment: 9 x 13-inch (22 x 33 cm) baking dish

1 Melt margarine over low heat in a 5-quart or larger saucepan. Add marshmallows, and stir. Let marshmallows melt completely, stirring occasionally. Add peach gelatin powder and stir to combine. Remove from heat.

2 Pour in rice cereal and stir until covered with marshmallow. Fold in dried peaches, if using. Turn out into a 9 × 13-inch (22 × 33 cm) baking dish that has been well coated with nonstick cooking spray. Push mixture down evenly with greased hands or spatula. Let cool.

3 Store in an airtight container on countertop and serve within 24 hours. Right before serving, spread whipped topping over treat mixture and cut into 2-inch (5 cm) squares.

Cherry Limeade Crispy Treats

Celebrate the flavors of summer with some cherry limeade crispy treats. Kool-aid and store-bought frosting make these treats super easy and quick to put together.

YIELD: 12 3-INCH (7 CM) SQUARES
TIME: 20 MINUTES ACTIVE,
20 MINUTES COOLING TIME
DIFFICULTY LEVEL: EASY

3 tbsp margarine
1 10-ounce (280 g) bag
    mini marshmallows
½ 0.16-ounce (4.6 g) packet
    cherry limeade Kool-Aid
6 cups (150 g) crisp rice cereal
1 16-ounce (250 g) container
    key lime frosting or green-
    tinted vanilla frosting
24 maraschino cherries
    (optional)

Equipment: 9 x 13-inch
(22 x 33 cm) baking dish

1 Melt margarine over low heat in a 5-quart or larger saucepan. Add marshmallows, and stir. Let marshmallows melt completely, stirring occasionally. Stir in Kool-Aid until completely combined. Remove from heat.

2 Pour in rice cereal and stir until covered with marshmallow. Turn out into a 9 × 13-inch (22 × 33 cm) baking dish that has been well coated with nonstick cooking spray. Push down evenly with greased hands or spatula. Let cool completely.

3 Store in an airtight container on countertop and serve within 24 hours. Just before serving, top treat mixture with key lime frosting and cut into 2-inch (5 cm) squares. If desired, finish off each treat with a maraschino cherry on top.

Everything but the Kitchen Sink Crispy Treats

．．．．．．．．．．．．．．

Pretzels, coconut, and three kinds of baking chips come together to tickle your taste buds with a medley of flavors. Feel free to experiment and incorporate your own favorite ingredients (nuts, for instance, work well).

YIELD: 24 2-INCH (5 CM) SQUARES
TIME: 30 MINUTES
DIFFICULTY LEVEL: EASY

⅓ cup (60 g) butterscotch chips

⅓ cup (60 g) chocolate chips

⅓ cup (60 g) white chocolate chips

⅓ cup (30 g) stick pretzels, broken into small pieces

¼ cup (18 g) sweetened shredded coconut

4 tbsp margarine

6½ cups (12 ounces [355 g]) mini marshmallows

6 cups (150 g) crisp rice cereal

Equipment: 9 x 13-inch (22 x 33 cm) baking dish

1 Freeze all of the baking chips at least 1 hour prior to preparing treats.

2 In a small mixing bowl, combine pretzels, all of the frozen chips, and coconut. Set aside.

3 Melt margarine over low heat in a 5-quart or larger saucepan. Add marshmallows and stir. Let marshmallows melt completely, stirring occasionally. Remove from heat.

4 Pour in rice cereal and stir until covered with marshmallow. Sprinkle in pretzel mixture. Stir until all ingredients are distributed throughout rice cereal mixture. Turn out into a 9 × 13-inch (22 × 33 cm) baking dish that has been well coated with nonstick cooking spray. Push down evenly with greased hands or spatula. Let cool.

5 Store in an airtight container and serve within 24 hours. Just before serving, cut into 2-inch (5 cm) squares.

Lemonade Treats with Strawberry Jam Frosting

• • • • • • • • • • • • •

Strawberry plus lemonade—need I say more? Using strawberry jam in the frosting cuts down on the prep time and means that you can make these summery treats any time of the year.

YIELD: 24 2-INCH (5 CM) SQUARES
TIME: 1 HOUR
DIFFICULTY LEVEL: EASY

Rice Cereal Mixture

3 tbsp margarine
1 10-ounce (280 g) bag
    mini marshmallows
⅓ cup (30 g) lemonade
    powdered drink mix
6 cups (150 g) crisp rice cereal

Frosting

1 cup or 2 sticks (225 g)
    butter, softened
1 tsp vanilla extract
⅓ cup (110 g) strawberry jam
2 cups (200 g) powdered
    sugar, sifted

Equipment: 9 x 13-inch
(22 x 33 cm) baking dish

1 Melt margarine over low heat in a 5-quart or larger saucepan. Add marshmallows, and stir. Let marshmallows melt completely, stirring occasionally. Remove from heat. Stir in lemonade drink mix.

2 Pour in rice cereal and stir until covered with marshmallow. Turn out into a greased 9 × 13-inch (22 × 33 cm) baking dish. Press down evenly with greased hands or spatula. Let cool.

3 While rice cereal mixture is cooling, make the strawberry frosting. With a hand mixer, beat butter on high speed for 3 minutes. Next, beat in vanilla and strawberry jam until incorporated. Finally, beat in powdered sugar 1 cup (100 g) at a time. Store frosting covered in refrigerator until ready to use.

4 Store treat mixture in an airtight container on countertop and serve within 24 hours. Just before serving, spread on frosting (plan to remove frosting from fridge about 20 to 30 minutes in advance so that it isn't too hard) and cut into 2-inch (5 cm) squares.

Cookies and Cream Crispy Treats

• • • • • • • • • • • • •

Cookies and cream is one of my favorite flavor combinations. It's no surprise that it makes a delicious rice crispy treat.

YIELD: 24 2-INCH (5 CM) SQUARES
TIME: 45 MINUTES
DIFFICULTY LEVEL: EASY

20 chocolate sandwich
    cookies
3 tbsp margarine
1 10-ounce (280 g) bag
    mini marshmallows
5 cups (125 g) crisp rice cereal
2 ounces (55 g) white
    almond bark

Equipment: 9 x 13-inch
(22 x 33 cm) baking dish

1 Place chocolate sandwich cookies in a plastic freezer bag and crush by hand or with a rolling pin. Leave some chunks larger than others.

2 Melt margarine over low heat in a 5-quart or larger saucepan. Add marshmallows, and stir. Let marshmallows melt completely, stirring occasionally. Remove from heat.

3 Add in rice cereal and stir until almost fully combined. Mix in ¾ of the crushed cookies.

4 Turn out rice cereal mixture into a 9 × 13-inch (22 × 33 cm) baking dish that has been well coated with nonstick cooking spray. While mixture is still warm, sprinkle remaining crushed cookies over top and gently press them into mixture.

5 Using a small microwave-safe bowl, heat white almond bark in microwave in 30-second increments until completely melted, stirring between each heating. (I recommend using High power level for first heating and switching to 50 percent power for subsequent heatings.) Using a spoon, drizzle melted almond bark over treat mixture. Let cool. Cut into 24 2-inch (5 cm) squares.

6 Store in an airtight container on countertop and serve within 24 hours. Cut into 2-inch (5 cm) squares just before serving.

S'mores Crispy Treats

Bring the taste of a campfire inside by whipping up a batch of these S'mores Crispy Treats. They're just as much fun to eat as the real deal.

YIELD: 16 2-INCH (5 CM) SQUARES
TIME: 45 MINUTES
DIFFICULTY LEVEL: EASY

2 tbsp margarine
2¾ cups (5 ounces [140 g])
  mini marshmallows
3 cups (75 g) crisp rice cereal
½ cup (50 g) graham cracker
  crumbs
1 7-ounce (200 g) jar
  marshmallow crème
½ cup (90 g) chocolate chips

Equipment: 2 9 x 9-inch
(22 x 22 cm) baking dishes

Treat Tip:
Cold crispy rice treats can get brittle and stick to the baking dish. Allow them to return to room temperature before cutting.

1 Melt margarine over low heat in a 5-quart or larger saucepan. Add marshmallows, and stir. Let marshmallows melt completely, stirring occasionally. Remove from heat.

2 Pour in rice cereal and graham cracker crumbs, and stir until covered with marshmallow. Divide mixture in half and turn out each half into a separate greased 9 × 9-inch baking dish. Push down evenly on both mixtures.

3 Spread marshmallow crème over one of the 9 × 9-inch layers of treat mixture. (If you're finding the marshmallow crème difficult to spread, warm it slightly.) Refrigerate for 10 minutes to allow marshmallow crème to set.

4 Using a microwave-safe bowl, heat chocolate chips in microwave in 30-second increments until completely melted, stirring between each heating. Overheating can cause chocolate to scorch, so heat only enough to get a smooth, velvety consistency. I recommend using High power level for first heating and switching to 50 percent power for subsequent heatings.

5 Spread melted chocolate over marshmallow crème. Return treat mixture to refrigerator for 10 minutes or until chocolate has set.

6 Turn out the second 9 × 9-inch layer of treat mixture on top of the chocolate layer. Store in an airtight container on countertop and serve within 24 hours. Just before serving, cut into 2-inch (5 cm) squares.

Piña Colada Crispy Treats

Transport your taste buds to an island paradise. Featuring pineapple and coconut in both the crispy base and the frosting, these enticing treats deliver double the tropical pleasure.

YIELD: 24 2-INCH (5 CM) SQUARES
TIME: 1 HOUR
DIFFICULTY LEVEL: INTERMEDIATE

Frosting

8 ounces (225 g) cream
 cheese, softened
¼ cup (60 ml) coconut milk
5 to 6 cups (500–600 g)
 powdered sugar
8 ounces (225 g) crushed
 pineapple, drained and
 as dry as possible

Rice Cereal Mixture

3 tbsp coconut oil
1 10-ounce (280 g) bag
 mini marshmallows
6 cups (150 g) crisp rice cereal
½ cup (75 g) chopped dried
 pineapple
½ cup (35 g) sweetened
 shredded coconut

Equipment: 9 x 13-inch
(22 x 33 cm) baking dish

1 First make the frosting. With a mixer, combine softened cream cheese and coconut milk until completely combined.

2 Add 1 cup (100 g) of the powdered sugar, mixing until completely combined. Continue to add powdered sugar in this manner, 1 cup at a time, until frosting has reached a thick, spreadable consistency. Fold in crushed pineapple. Refrigerate covered until ready to serve.

3 Next, make the rice cereal mixture. Heat coconut oil over low heat in a 5-quart or larger saucepan. Add marshmallows, and stir. Let marshmallows melt completely, stirring occasionally. Remove from heat.

4 Pour in rice cereal and stir until covered with marshmallow. Fold in dried pineapple and shredded coconut. Spread into a 9 × 13-inch (22 × 33 cm) baking dish that has been well coated with nonstick cooking spray. Push mixture down evenly with greased hands or spatula. Let cool.

5 Store in an airtight container on countertop and serve within 24 hours. Right before serving, top with pineapple-coconut frosting (plan to remove frosting from fridge about 20 to 30 minutes in advance so that it isn't too hard) and cut into 2-inch (5 cm) squares.

Chocolate-Hazelnut Crispy Treats

Chocolate-hazelnut spread is all the rage, and for good reason—it's delicious! In this recipe, it is paired with chocolate crisp rice cereal to create the ultimate chocolate experience. If you prefer a subtler chocolate flavor, simply use regular crisp rice cereal instead.

YIELD: 24 2-INCH (5 CM) SQUARES
TIME: 30 MINUTES
DIFFICULTY LEVEL: EASY

3 tbsp margarine

1 10-ounce (280 g) bag mini marshmallows

½ cup (140 g) chocolate-hazelnut spread

6 cups (150 g) chocolate crisp rice cereal

½ cup (60 g) roasted hazelnuts, chopped (optional)

Equipment: 9 x 13-inch (22 x 33 cm) baking dish

1 Melt margarine over low heat in a 5-quart or larger saucepan. Add marshmallows, and stir. Let marshmallows melt completely, stirring occasionally. Add in chocolate-hazelnut spread and stir to combine. Remove from heat.

2 Pour in chocolate rice cereal and stir until covered with marshmallow. Spread into greased 9 × 13-inch (22 × 33 cm) baking dish. Push down evenly with greased hands or spatula. If desired, sprinkle chopped hazelnuts over treat mixture and press down gently. Let cool.

3 Store in an airtight container on countertop, and serve within 24 hours. Cut into 2-inch (5 cm) squares right before serving.

Neapolitan Crispy Treats

Layers of chocolate, vanilla, and strawberry treats stacked up look just as good as they taste. This recipe is easy to make and delivers a strong visual punch.

YIELD: 24 2-INCH (5 CM) SQUARES
TIME: 1 HOUR
DIFFICULTY LEVEL: EASY

6 tbsp margarine
8¼ cups (15 ounces [420 g]) mini marshmallows
3 cups (75 g) chocolate crisp rice cereal
1 tsp vanilla extract
6 cups (150 g) crisp rice cereal
2 tbsp strawberry gelatin powder

Equipment: 9 x 13-inch (22 x 33 cm) baking dish

1 Start by making the chocolate layer. Melt 2 tablespoons of the margarine over low heat in a saucepan. Add 2¾ cups (140 g) of the mini marshmallows, and stir. Let marshmallows melt completely, stirring occasionally. Remove from heat. Pour in chocolate rice cereal and stir until covered with marshmallow. Turn out into a greased 9 × 13-inch (22 × 33 cm) baking dish and press down into a uniform layer.

2 Next make the vanilla layer. Melt 2 tablespoons of the margarine over low heat in a saucepan. Add 2¾ cups (140 g) of the mini marshmallows, and stir. Let marshmallows melt completely, stirring occasionally. Add in vanilla extract and stir to combine. Remove from heat. Pour in half of the plain rice cereal and stir until covered with marshmallow. Add vanilla rice cereal mixture on top of chocolate layer and press flat with greased hands or spatula.

3 Finally make the strawberry layer. Repeat step 2, but instead of adding vanilla extract, add the strawberry gelatin powder. Spread strawberry rice cereal layer on top of vanilla layer. Let cool.

4 Store in an airtight container and serve within 24 hours. Just before serving, cut into 2-inch (5 cm) squares.

German Chocolate Crispy Treats

. . . .

German chocolate cake isn't the same without coconut-pecan frosting, and these treats are no different. You can substitute store-bought frosting if you are in a hurry, but this homemade version is worth the effort.

YIELD: 24 2-INCH (5 CM) SQUARES
TIME: 1½ HOURS
DIFFICULTY LEVEL: INTERMEDIATE

Frosting
4 egg yolks
1 14-ounce (425 ml) can condensed milk
1½ tsp vanilla extract
1½ cups (300 g) sugar
¾ cups (170 g) butter
2½ (175 g) cups shredded coconut
1½ cups (185 g) chopped pecans

Rice Cereal Mixture
3 tbsp margarine
1 10-ounce (280 g) bag mini marshmallows
4 ounces (115 g) German chocolate baking chocolate, chopped
6 cups (150 g) chocolate rice cereal

Equipment: 9 x 13-inch (22 x 33 cm) baking dish

1 First make the frosting. Whisk together egg yolks, condensed milk, and vanilla in a saucepan over medium heat. Add in sugar and butter. Cook over medium heat, stirring constantly until mixture thickens (about 10 to 15 minutes). Remove from heat. Stir in coconut and pecans. Set aside until completely cooled.

2 Next make the rice cereal mixture. Melt margarine in a 5-quart or larger saucepan over low heat. Add marshmallows, and stir. Let marshmallows melt completely, stirring occasionally. Add German chocolate and stir until melted. Remove from heat.

3 Pour in chocolate rice cereal and stir until covered with marshmallow. Turn out into a greased 9 × 13-inch (22 × 33 cm) baking dish, and push down evenly with greased hands or spatula. Let cool. Top with cooled coconut pecan frosting and cut into 2-inch (5 cm) squares.

Turtle Crispy Treats

No, I'm not talking about the shelled animals that grace land and sea. Rather, these are the kind made with chocolate, pecans, and caramel. Not only is this layered version positively scrumptious, it's one of my favorite recipes.

YIELD: 16 1½-INCH (3.75 CM)
SQUARES
TIME: 45 MINUTES
DIFFICULTY LEVEL: INTERMEDIATE

Rice Cereal Mixture

2 tbsp margarine
2¾ cups (5 ounces [140 g]) mini marshmallows
3 cups (75 g) crisp rice cereal

Filling

¾ cup (75 g) pecan halves
1 11-ounce (311 g) bag caramel bits
1 cup (225 g) chocolate chips

Topping

½ cup (60 g) caramel bits
1½ tsp milk
½ cup (115 g) chocolate chips
½ cup (60 g) chopped pecan pieces

Equipment: 2 9 x 9-inch (22 x 22 cm) baking dishes

1 First make the rice cereal mixture. Melt margarine over low heat in a 5-quart or larger saucepan. Add marshmallows, and stir. Let marshmallows melt completely, stirring occasionally. Remove from heat.

2 Pour in rice cereal and stir until completely combined. Divide mixture in half and press each half into a separate greased 9 × 9-inch baking dish.

3 For the filling, lay pecan halves end to end in a single layer on top of rice cereal mixture in one of the baking dishes, and press down slightly. Melt caramel bits in a saucepan according to package directions. Carefully pour melted caramel over the pecan halves. Refrigerate for 5 minutes or until caramel has set.

4 Using a microwave-safe bowl, heat chocolate chips in the microwave in 30-second increments until completely melted, stirring between each heating. Note that overheating can cause chocolate to scorch and separate, so take care to heat chocolate only long enough to get a smooth, velvety consistency. I recommend using High power level for first heating and switching to 50 percent power for subsequent heatings.

5 Spread thin layer of melted chocolate over the caramel. Refrigerate at least 10 minutes to firm up chocolate.

6 Remove rice cereal mixture from the second baking dish and gently place it on top of the chocolate layer. If the sides of the baking dish are angled, you may need to gently stretch the mixture to reach the edges.

7 For the topping, melt caramel and milk together in a small saucepan and drizzle over top layer of crispy treat mixture. Melt chocolate chips in microwave (in same manner as in step 4) and drizzle over caramel. Sprinkle with chopped pecans. Let chocolate and caramel set.

8 Store in an airtight container on countertop and serve within 24 hours. Shortly before serving, cut into 1½-inch (3.75 cm) squares.

Cherry Chip Treats

The cherry chips studding these crispy treats not only enhance the taste but take the visual appeal up a notch, too. Feel free to experiment with different cake mix flavors.

YIELD: 24 2-INCH (5 CM) SQUARES
TIME: 30 MINUTES
DIFFICULTY LEVEL: EASY

1 cup (60 g) cherry flavored baking chips
3 tbsp margarine
1 10-ounce (280 g) bag mini marshmallows
⅓ cup (30 g) white cake mix, sifted to remove clumps
6 cups (150 g) crisp rice cereal

Equipment: 9 x 13-inch (22 x 33 cm) baking dish

1 Place cherry chips in the freezer for at least 1 hour prior to preparing treats.

2 Melt margarine over low heat in a 5-quart or larger saucepan. Add marshmallows, and stir. Let marshmallows melt completely, stirring occasionally. Remove from heat. Stir in white cake mix.

3 Pour in rice cereal and stir until covered with marshmallow mixture. Let mixture cool in saucepan for 3 minutes. Remove cherry chips from freezer and fold into warm treats. Turn out into a greased 9 × 13-inch (22 × 33 cm) baking dish. Press down with greased hands or spatula.

4 Store in an airtight container and serve within 24 hours. Shortly before serving, cut into 2-inch (5 cm) squares.

Pumpkin Spice Crispy Treats with Cinnamon Cream Cheese Frosting

• • • . . • • • . • . • • •

Pumpkin is one of my favorite flavors, and I could eat it all the time. But the cinnamon cream cheese frosting that tops these pumpkin delights gives them a touch of decadence worthy of a special occasion.

YIELD: 24 2-INCH (5 CM) SQUARES
TIME: 1 HOUR
DIFFICULTY LEVEL: EASY

Frosting

8 ounces (225 g) cream cheese, room temperature
¼ cup (55 g) butter, room temperature
1 tsp vanilla extract
2 tsp ground cinnamon
2 to 3 cups (200–300 g) powdered sugar

Rice Cereal Mixture

3 tbsp margarine
1 10-ounce (280 g) bag mini marshmallows
1 3.4-ounce (96 g) packet Jell-o Pumpkin Spice instant pudding mix
6 cups (150 g) crisp rice cereal

Equipment: 9 x 13-inch (22 x 33 cm) baking dish

1 First make the frosting: With a mixer, cream together cream cheese, butter, vanilla, and cinnamon. Add 1 cup (100 g) powdered sugar and mix until combined. Continue adding powdered sugar, 1 cup at a time and mixing in between, until desired thickness is reached, up to 3 cups. Refrigerate covered until ready to use.

2 Melt margarine over low heat in a 5-quart or larger saucepan. Add marshmallows, and stir. Let marshmallows melt completely, stirring occasionally. Mix in pumpkin spice pudding mix. Remove from heat.

3 Pour in rice cereal and stir until covered with marshmallow mixture. Spread rice cereal mixture into a 9 × 13-inch (22 × 33 cm) baking dish that has been well coated with nonstick cooking spray. Press down evenly with greased hands or spatula. Let cool.

4 Store in an airtight container on countertop and serve within 24 hours. Just before serving, top with cinnamon frosting (plan to remove frosting from fridge about 20 to 30 minutes in advance so that it isn't too hard) and cut into 2-inch (5 cm) squares.

Cookie Dough Crispy Treats

This egg-free cookie dough is safe to eat raw and so delicious. Freezing the cookie dough helps it stay in shape when added to the warm rice crispy mixture. You'll definitely be coming back for seconds of these.

YIELD: 24 2-INCH (5 CM) SQUARES
TIME: 40 MINUTES ACTIVE.
1 TO 3 HOURS WAITING
DIFFICULTY LEVEL: INTERMEDIATE

Cookie Dough

½ cup or 1 stick (113 g)
   butter, softened
¾ cup (170 g) packed light
   brown sugar
2 tsp vanilla extract
1 cup (100 g) flour
2 tbsp milk
½ tsp salt
⅓ cup (60 g) mini chocolate
   chips

Rice Cereal Mixture

3 tbsp margarine
1 10-ounce (280 g) bag
   mini marshmallows
5 cups (125 g) crisp rice cereal

Equipment: 9 x 13-inch
(22 x 33 cm) baking dish,
parchment paper

1 First make the cookie dough. Cream together butter, brown sugar, and vanilla with a mixer. Add in flour, milk, and salt and mix until a dough has formed. Fold in chocolate chips. Spread cookie dough into a thin layer on a baking sheet covered with parchment paper. Freeze for 1 to 3 hours. Cut into small ½" (1.27 cm) squares. Return to freezer.

2 Next make the rice cereal mixture. Melt margarine over low heat in a 5-quart or larger saucepan. Add marshmallows, and stir. Let marshmallows melt completely, stirring occasionally. Remove from heat.

3 Add in rice cereal and stir until covered with marshmallow. Once ingredients are combined, fold in about ¾ of the frozen cookie dough chunks. Turn out into a well-greased 9 × 13-inch (22 × 33 cm) baking dish. Press remaining cookie dough chunks into the top of the treat mixture.

4 Store in an airtight container on countertop and serve within 24 hours. Just before serving, cut into 2-inch (5 cm) squares.

Horchata Crispy Treats

• • • • • • • • • • • •

While the ingredients vary according to region, *horchata* is a popular drink in Latin American countries, where it often features rice, milk, and cinnamon. Though the tasty beverage is typically made from scratch, there are now powdered mixes available to concoct the yummy drink. Check the Latin American section of your grocery store or the aisle where powdered drink mixes are sold.

YIELD: 24 2-INCH (5 CM) SQUARES
TIME: 30 MINUTES
DIFFICULTY LEVEL: EASY

3 tbsp margarine
1 10-ounce (280 g) bag
  mini marshmallows
¼ cup (25 g) horchata drink
  mix powder
1 tsp ground cinnamon
6 cups (150 g) crisp rice
  cereal

Equipment: 9 x 13-inch
(22 x 33 cm) baking dish

1 Melt margarine over low heat in a 5-quart or larger saucepan. Add marshmallows, and stir. Let marshmallows melt completely, stirring occasionally. Add in horchata mix and cinnamon. Stir to combine. Remove from heat.

2 Pour in rice cereal and stir until covered with marshmallow. Turn out into a 9 × 13-inch (22 × 33 cm) baking dish that has been well coated with nonstick cooking spray. Push down evenly with greased hands or spatula. Let cool.

3 Store in an airtight container on countertop and serve within 24 hours. Shortly before serving, cut into 2-inch (5 cm) squares.

Chapter Six

Alternative Crispy Treats

Cinnamon Roll Treats

Cinnamon rolls can take hours to prepare, but this crispy treat version is ready in just over an hour. Plus the brown sugar frosting is dreamy!

YIELD: 18 CINNAMON ROLLS
TIME: 1¼ HOURS
DIFFICULTY LEVEL: INTERMEDIATE

Brown Sugar Frosting

½ cup (112 g) butter
1 packed cup (225 g) dark brown sugar
½ cup (120 ml) milk
2 cups (200 g) powdered sugar, sifted
1 tbsp warm water, if needed

Rice Cereal Mixture

3 tbsp margarine
1 10-ounce (280 g) bag mini marshmallows
1 tbsp ground cinnamon
6 cups (150 g) crisp rice cereal

Vanilla Glaze

¼ cup (55 g) butter
3 cups (300 g) powdered sugar
½ tsp vanilla extract
¼ cup (60 ml) milk

Equipment: 13 x 18-inch (33 x 46 cm) baking sheet

1 Start making the frosting. In a saucepan, melt butter. Add in dark brown sugar and bring to a boil. Turn heat down to medium-low and continue to boil for 2 minutes, stirring continuously. Add milk and boil, still stirring continuously. Remove from heat and allow to cool until lukewarm, stirring occasionally.

2 While brown sugar mixture is cooling, make the rice cereal mixture. Melt margarine over low heat in a 5-quart or larger saucepan. Add marshmallows, and stir. Let marshmallows melt completely, stirring occasionally. Add cinnamon and stir to combine. Remove from heat.

3 Pour in rice cereal and stir until covered with marshmallow. Turn out onto your baking sheet that has been well coated with nonstick cooking spray. Push down evenly, making sure the layer completely covers the baking sheet. Set aside.

4 Once the brown sugar mixture has cooled to lukewarm, slowly add in the sifted 2 cups of powdered sugar to finish making the frosting. If the frosting gets too thick, add 1 tablespoon warm water to thin.

5 Spread frosting over entire surface of cinnamon crispy mixture. Starting on the long side of the baking sheet, slowly roll frosted treat mixture into a log shape. Set aside.

6 Next make the vanilla glaze. Melt butter on stove top, then remove from heat. Add powdered sugar. Slowly add vanilla and milk, stirring as you go to desired glaze consistency. Drizzle the treats with the glaze before serving.

Brownie Goody Bars

You can't go wrong when you combine peanut butter and chocolate. Plus, these bars come together quickly and easily, which make them ideal for busy moms.

YIELD: 12 BARS
TIME: 25 MINUTES ACTIVE,
1 ½ HOURS SETTING TIME
DIFFICULTY LEVEL: EASY

1 18.3-ounce (286 g) or family size package fudge brownie mix
¼ cup (60 ml) water
½ cup (120 ml) vegetable oil
2 eggs
1 16-ounce (250 g) container vanilla frosting
3 cups (75 g) crisp rice cereal
1 cup (250 g) creamy peanut butter
1 cup (175 g) semisweet chocolate chips

Equipment: 9 x 13-inch (22 x 33 cm) baking dish

1 Heat oven to 350°F (180°C). Grease bottom of a baking dish. Combine brownie mix, water, oil, and eggs in a medium bowl until well blended. Spread into baking dish. Bake 25 to 30 minutes or until toothpick inserted into brownie 2 inches (5 cm) from side of baking dish comes out clean or almost clean. Cool completely, about 1 hour.

2 Spread frosting over brownies and refrigerate covered while you prepare cereal mixture. Measure crisp rice cereal into a large bowl and set aside. Melt peanut butter and chocolate chips in a saucepan over low heat, stirring constantly. When mixture is melted and completely combined, pour over cereal in bowl and stir to combine. Spread cereal mixture over frosted brownies. Cool completely before cutting.

3 Store treats in an airtight container at room temperature and serve within 24 hours. To keep treats longer, refrigerate for 2 to 3 days. Allow refrigerated treats to sit at room temperature for 20 to 30 minutes before serving.

Key Lime Cheesecake Bars with Coconut Crispy Treat Crust

Crispy treats can make a great base for other sweet concoctions. In this recipe, the coconut crispy treat "crust" adds a delightfully unexpected element to already hard-to-improve-upon key lime cheesecake bars.

YIELD: 24 2-INCH (5 CM) SQUARES
TIME: 30 MINUTES ACTIVE,
30 MINUTES WAITING
DIFFICULTY LEVEL: INTERMEDIATE

Crust

2 tbsp coconut oil
2¾ cups (5 ounces [140 g]) mini marshmallows
3 cups (75 g) crisp rice cereal
¼ cup (18 g) sweetened shredded coconut

Filling

½ cup (120 ml) key lime juice
¼ cup (50 g) sugar
2 tsp unflavored gelatin
2 8-ounce (225 g) packages cream cheese, room temperature
1 14-ounce (425 ml) can sweetened condensed milk
½ tsp vanilla extract

Equipment: 9 x 13-inch (22 x 33 cm) baking dish

1 Heat coconut oil in a saucepan over low heat until liquid. Add marshmallows, and stir. Let marshmallows melt completely, stirring occasionally. Remove from heat.

2 Stir in crisp rice cereal and shredded coconut until completely incorporated. Turn out into a greased 9 × 13-inch (22 × 33 cm) baking dish. Press down firmly to make a thin crust. Set aside.

3 Heat lime juice over low heat in a saucepan. Whisk in sugar and gelatin. Heat until sugar and gelatin are completely dissolved. Remove from heat and set aside.

4 In a large mixing bowl, beat cream cheese with a hand mixer on high for 4 minutes. Add sweetened condensed milk and beat until combined. Beat in lime gelatin and vanilla. Pour cheesecake filling over crispy treat crust and refrigerate 30 minutes or until filling has set.

5 Just before serving, cut into 2-inch (5 cm) squares. Over time, cheesecake filling may make the crispy treats soggy. Enjoy within 24 hours.

Sweet Trail Mix

This sweet trail mix would be great for serving at a party or munching on during a movie. You can customize the colors used to coordinate with almost any theme or holiday.

YIELD: 8 CUPS TRAIL MIX
TIME: 30 MINUTES ACTIVE.
20 MINUTES DRYING TIME
DIFFICULTY LEVEL: EASY

2 tbsp margarine

2¾ cups (5 ounces [140 g]) mini marshmallows

Gel food coloring of choice (optional)

3 cups (75 g) crisp rice cereal

2 cups (115 g) round or mini pretzel twists

1 cup (210 g) chocolate candies

6 ounces (170 g) almond bark or colored candy melts

Equipment: Greased baking sheet or sheet of parchment paper

1 Melt margarine over low heat in a 3-quart or larger saucepan. Add marshmallows, and stir. Let marshmallows melt completely, stirring occasionally. Remove from heat. For colored crispy treats, add a few drops of gel food coloring and stir to combine. Continue adding gel coloring until desired shade is reached.

2 Stir in crisp rice cereal until covered with marshmallow. Turn out onto a greased baking sheet or sheet of parchment paper, spreading mixture all over tray. The mixture doesn't need to be flat, nor does it all need to stay together—just spread it nice and thin. Sprinkle pretzels and chocolate candies over top of mixture.

3 Using a microwave-safe dish, heat almond bark in microwave in 30-second increments until melted, stirring between each heating. (I recommend using High power level for first heating and switching to 50 percent power for subsequent heatings.) Drizzle melted almond bark over trail mix. Once topping is dry, break trail mix into bite-size pieces. The candies and pretzels may or may not stick to the crispy treats.

4 Store in an airtight bag and serve within 24 hours.

Crispy Ice Cream Sandwich Treats

· · · · . . . . . . · · · · ·

Ice cream sandwiches are a great way to cool off in the summer. Make your own novel version with crispy treats standing in for the traditional soft cookie.

YIELD: 12 SANDWICHES
TIME: 45 MINUTES ACTIVE.
4+ HOURS WAITING
DIFFICULTY LEVEL: INTERMEDIATE

½ gallon (3.8 L) vanilla
　ice cream
3 tbsp margarine
1 10-ounce (280 g) bag
　mini marshmallows
¼ cup (25 g) cocoa powder
6 cups (150 g) chocolate
　crisp rice cereal

Equipment: Parchment paper, three 9 x 13-inch (22 x 33 cm) baking dishes, 4-inch (10 cm) square or 2 x 4-inch (5 x 10 cm) rectangle cookie cutter (optional)

1　Remove vanilla ice cream from freezer and let sit at room temperature for 20 minutes or until very soft and spreadable. Cut a piece of parchment paper to 9 × 20 (22 × 51 cm) inches and place in a 9 × 13-inch (22 × 33 cm) baking dish, leaving a few inches of paper hanging out on each end. Spread vanilla ice cream into an even layer in baking dish. Place in freezer for at least 3 hours; overnight is best.

2　Melt margarine over low heat in a 5-quart or larger saucepan. Add marshmallows, and stir. Let marshmallows melt completely, stirring occasionally. Add cocoa powder and stir until completely combined. Remove from heat.

3　Pour in chocolate crisp rice cereal and stir until covered with marshmallow. Divide treat mixture evenly between two 9 × 13-inch (22 × 33 cm) baking dishes that have been coated with nonstick cooking spray. Coat clean hands with nonstick cooking spray and press mixture into a thin layer that completely covers bottom of both baking dishes. Let cool for at least 1 hour.

4　Using a knife or cookie cutter, cut treat mixtures into pieces of equal size and shape. Remove ice cream from freezer. Run a knife around edges of 9 × 13-inch (22 × 33 cm) baking dish to loosen ice cream. Pull up parchment paper ends and remove ice cream from baking dish. Cut ice cream into same size and shape as the crispy treats, then sandwich between two treats. Serve immediately.

Unfried Ice Cream

All the deliciousness and crunch of traditional fried ice cream without the extra calories or the hassle of using a fryer.

YIELD: 8 TO 12 SCOOPS
OF ICE CREAM
TIME: 20 MINUTES
DIFFICULTY LEVEL: EASY

4 cups (100 g) crisp rice cereal

1 tbsp ground cinnamon

½ gallon (3.8 L) vanilla ice cream

Toppings of your choice, such as chocolate sauce, whipped cream, maraschino cherries, etc.

Equipment: Ice cream scoop

1 Put crisp rice cereal in a gallon plastic bag and lightly crush. Add cinnamon, seal bag, and shake to combine. Pour crushed cereal into a medium bowl.

2 Scoop some ice cream out of container with an ice cream scooper and immediately roll ball in crushed cereal. Place coated ball on a cold baking sheet (this will prevent ice cream from melting too quickly). Repeat for rest of half gallon.

3 Serve the same day. If not enjoying immediately, store in airtight container in freezer until ready to serve. Just before serving, add chocolate sauce, whipped cream, a cherry, or any of your favorite toppings.

Treat Tip:

Dip the ice cream scoop in hot water to get through frozen hard ice cream. Be sure to dry the scoop right away, as water left on the scoop will form ice crystals.

Crispy Treat Fondue

Fondue is a fun activity when entertaining friends and family. With this version, guests can envelop their treats in a heated dipping "sauce" of vanilla frosting and then finish the scrumptious morsels off with their favorite toppings.

YIELD: APPROXIMATELY 36
CRISPY TREATS
TIME: 30 MINUTES
DIFFICULTY LEVEL: EASY

3 tbsp margarine
1 10-ounce (280 g) bag
    mini marshmallows
6 cups (150 g) crisp rice cereal
1 16-ounce (450 g) tub
    vanilla frosting
2 tbsp milk, plus more
    if needed
Toppings of choice, such
    as sprinkles, miniature
    chocolate chips, crushed
    Oreos, chopped nuts

Equipment: Parchment paper (optional), 1- to 1½-quart slow cooker, fondue forks or 10-inch (25 cm) skewers

1 Melt margarine over low heat in a 5-quart or larger saucepan. Add marshmallows, and stir. Let marshmallows melt completely, stirring occasionally. Remove from heat.

2 Stir in crisp rice cereal until covered with marshmallow. As soon as mixture is cool enough to handle, form into 1-inch (2.5 cm) balls with greased hands. Set treats on a greased baking sheet or sheet of parchment paper, and let cool completely.

3 Before party time, put frosting in slow cooker and begin heating over low heat. Stir in milk to thin to a dipping consistency, starting with 2 tablespoons and adding more if necessary. Heat on low until frosting is ready for dipping. After that, keep slow cooker on warm setting, stirring occasionally to keep smooth.

4 To serve, set out crispy treats, fondue forks, and all toppings, and tell your guests to dip away. Be sure to provide spoons for sprinkling toppings on dipped treats.

Rainbow Crispy Layer Cake

• • • • • • • • • • • • • • •

This dessert looks pretty unassuming from the outside, but what a surprise when the cake is cut and six layers of crispy treats—each a different color—are revealed! I recommend using at least two round baking pans when making this dazzling dessert; that way, you can make two layers at a time.

YIELD: SERVES 24
TIME: 2 HOURS ACTIVE.
1 HOUR WAITING
DIFFICULTY LEVEL: ADVANCED

12 tbsp margarine

30 ounces (840 g) mini marshmallows

Purple, blue, green, yellow, orange, and red gel food coloring

18 cups (450 g) crisp rice cereal

12 cups (4 batches) Buttercream Frosting (see page ix)

Rainbow sprinkles

Equipment: 9-inch (22 cm) round baking pan(s), parchment paper, cake stand or cake turntable, offset spatula, wood skewers (optional)

1 For the cake, you will be making 6 half batches of crispy treats in different colors. Start with the bottom layer, purple, then work your way up to the top in the following order to mimic a rainbow: blue, green, yellow, orange, red.

2 Melt 2 tablespoons of the margarine over low heat in a 3-quart or larger saucepan. Add 2¾ cups (140 g) of the marshmallows, and stir. Let marshmallows melt completely, stirring occasionally. Remove from heat. Add a few drops of purple gel food coloring and stir to combine. Continue adding gel coloring until desired shade is reached.

3 Stir in 3 cups (75 g) crisp rice cereal until covered with marshmallow. Turn out into a greased 9-inch (22 cm) round baking pan. With greased hands, press into an even layer. Let cool completely. Once layer is cool, invert pan and remove. Set purple layer on a sheet of parchment paper until ready to stack. Repeat steps 2 and 3 for the remaining 5 layers of colored treats.

4 Place purple treat layer, with the flatter side up, in the center of a cake stand or turntable (the latter will make icing easier). Spread a layer of buttercream frosting over top of purple layer, then add the blue layer. Continue to

stack all of the layers in this fashion, flatter side up and frosting in between, arranging them in the order presented in step 1.

5 Once all layers have been stacked, frost the top and sides. Place a large amount of frosting on top of cake and start spreading it around with an offset spatula. As top begins to even out, push frosting over sides. The frosting will need to be pretty thick to cover treats and achieve a smooth appearance. Keep adding frosting as needed until entire cake is covered. If you are using a turntable, hold spatula still and turn cake to get an even, smooth look. When frosting is as smooth as you can get it, cover top of cake with rainbow sprinkles.

6 To serve, cut cake with a serrated knife in a very slow sawing motion, as top layers may want to slide around. To prevent sliding, you can push some wooden skewers down into the cake before slicing for added leverage. As with any cake, the first slice is the most challenging; after that, it is much easier to cut. Store in an airtight container in the refrigerator and serve within 24 hours.

Treat Tip:
If the layers are stacked before they are cool, they may spread. If any layers of the cake end up wider than the others, trim them down with a serrated knife once they are stacked.

Crispy No-Bake Granola Bars

Skip out on the preservatives and make your own granola bars at home. This is a great recipe you can customize with your favorite ingredients.

YIELD: 10 TO 12 1½ X 4-INCH (3.75 X 10 CM) GRANOLA BARS
TIME: 20 MINUTES ACTIVE.
1 TO 2 HOURS DRYING TIME
DIFFICULTY LEVEL: INTERMEDIATE

1 cup (80 g) quick-cook oats
1 cup (25 g) crisp rice cereal
¼ cup (30 g) dried sweetened cranberries
¼ cup (32 g) sliced almonds
¼ cup (55 g) butter
¼ cup (85 g) honey
⅓ cup (75 g) brown sugar
½ tsp vanilla extract
¼ cup (44 g) miniature chocolate chips (optional)

Equipment: 8 x 8-inch (20 x 20 cm) baking dish, parchment paper

1 In a mixing bowl, mix together oats, crisp rice cereal, cranberries, and almonds. Set aside.

2 In a saucepan, heat butter, honey, and brown sugar over medium-high heat. Once mixture comes to a gentle boil, reduce heat to low and cook for 2 more minutes. The mixture needs to bubble continuously for a full 2 minutes, so if necessary, turn heat up slightly to keep it going. Stir in vanilla.

3 Pour hot mixture over dry ingredients and stir until everything is coated. Pour granola bar mixture into an 8 × 8-inch (20 × 20 cm) baking dish that has been coated with nonstick cooking spray and press down firmly into an even layer. If using chocolate chips, sprinkle them on now and gently press them into mixture.

4 Allow granola bars to cool for 1 to 2 hours. Cut into bars and store, wrapped in parchment paper, in an airtight container. Enjoy within 2 to 3 days.

Peanut Butter Crispy Cups

· · · · · · · · · · · · · · · · ·

Peanut butter cups are always a crowd favorite and this crispy treat version is sure to please.

YIELD: 24 CUPS
TIME: 45 MINUTES ACTIVE, 1 HOUR
20 MINUTES SETTING TIME
DIFFICULTY LEVEL: INTERMEDIATE

1½ tbsp softened butter
½ cup (125 g) peanut butter
¾ cup (75 g) powdered sugar
3 tbsp margarine
1 10-ounce (280 g) bag
   mini marshmallows
6 cups (150 g) crisp rice cereal
4 ounces (115 g) chocolate
   almond bark

Equipment: Mini muffin pan

1 Heat butter and peanut butter in a small saucepan over low heat. Stir occasionally until completely melted. Remove from heat. Slowly add powdered sugar and incorporate until a pliable mass has formed. Wrap peanut butter filling in plastic wrap and refrigerate for 1 hour.

2 Melt margarine over low heat in a 5-quart or larger saucepan. Add marshmallows, and stir. Let marshmallows melt completely, stirring occasionally. Remove from heat. Stir in crispy rice cereal until covered with marshmallow.

3 Spray mini muffin pan with nonstick cooking spray. Press small amount of crispy treat mixture into bottom of each muffin cavity and halfway up sides to form a cup. Next, add a small amount of peanut butter filling in middle of cup. Top with additional crispy treat mixture and press down, making sure filling is completely surrounded by crispy mixture. Remove crispy cups from mini muffin pan and place on greased baking sheet.

4 Using a microwave-safe dish, heat chocolate almond bark in the microwave in 30-second increments until melted, stirring between each heating. (I recommend using High power level for first heating and switching to 50 percent power for subsequent heatings.) Drizzle almond bark over peanut butter cups, and let harden. Store in an airtight container and serve within 24 hours.

Fruit Pizza with Crispy Crust

• • • • • • • • • • • • •

Fruit pizza is the perfect dessert to take to a summer picnic or potluck. You can save some time and energy by skipping the sugar cookie crust and making a rice crispy crust instead.

YIELD: 10 SLICES
TIME: 1½ HOURS
DIFFICULTY LEVEL: EASY

8 ounces (225 g) cream cheese, room temperature
¼ cup or ½ stick (57 g) butter, softened
1 tsp vanilla extract
2 to 3 cups (200–300 g) powdered sugar
3 tbsp margarine
1 10-ounce (280 g) bag mini marshmallows
6 cups (150 g) crisp rice cereal
Fresh fruit, such as strawberries, blueberries, bananas

Equipment: 12-inch (30 cm) pizza pan

1 Cream together cream cheese, butter, and vanilla. Add powdered sugar 1 cup (100 g) at a time, until desired thickness is reached, up to 3 cups (300 g). Set aside.

2 Melt margarine over low heat in a 5-quart or larger saucepan. Add marshmallows, and stir. Let marshmallows melt completely, stirring occasionally. Remove from heat. Pour in rice cereal and stir until covered with marshmallow.

3 Turn out crispy mixture onto a 12-inch (30 cm) pizza pan that has been well coated with nonstick cooking spray. Push down evenly with greased hands. Let cool.

4 Spread cream cheese frosting over top of crispy treat base, leaving a small, uncovered crispy treat border around edge. Decorate top of pizza with sliced fruit. Refrigerate, if not serving immediately. If refrigerated, let pizza sit at room temperature for about 10 minutes before slicing and serving. Make and serve same day.

Crispy Crunchy Chocolate Bark

• • • • • • • • • • • •

It only takes two ingredients to make a delicious crispy chocolate bark. This would be a great addition to your holiday goody plate.

YIELD: 1 POUND (455 G)
CRISPY BARK
TIME: 15 MINUTES ACTIVE,
20 MINUTES SETTING TIME
DIFFICULTY: EASY

1 pound (455 g) chocolate
    almond bark
3 cups (75 g) crisp rice cereal

Equipment: Parchment
paper

1 Heat almond bark in a small saucepan over medium-low heat. Stir occasionally to prevent scorching. Alternatively, melt almond bark in microwave, following package instructions.

2 Pour melted chocolate almond bark onto a baking sheet lined with parchment paper. Sprinkle crisp rice cereal over chocolate, and gently stir to coat. Spread chocolate-cereal mixture into an even layer with a mixing spoon. Allow to set completely.

3 Once almond bark has set, break into bite-size pieces. Store in an airtight container, and enjoy within 5 days.

Crispy Cannoli Treats

This crispy treat version of the classic Italian dessert is stuffed with a zesty, chocolate-studded ricotta filling.

YIELD: APPROXIMATELY 12 CANNOLI
TIME: 45 MINUTES, PLUS
30 MINUTES WAIT
DIFFICULTY LEVEL: INTERMEDIATE

15 ounces (425 g) whole milk ricotta cheese

Zest from 1 small lemon or orange

⅓ cup (58 g) miniature chocolate chips

3 tbsp margarine

1 10-ounce (280 g) bag mini marshmallows

½ tsp ground cinnamon

6 cups (150 g) crisp rice cereal

Equipment: 3- to 3½-inch (7.5–8.75 cm) circle cookie cutter, pastry bag

1 Drain ricotta cheese in a strainer set over a bowl for 30 minutes to remove any excess water. Stir together ricotta, citrus zest, and ¼ cup (45 g) of the miniature chocolate chips to make the cannoli filling. Refrigerate until ready to use.

2 Melt margarine over low heat in a 5-quart or larger saucepan. Add marshmallows, and stir. Let marshmallows melt completely, stirring occasionally. Remove from heat. Add cinnamon and stir.

3 Pour in crisp rice cereal and stir until covered with marshmallow. Turn out onto a greased baking sheet. With greased hands, press into an even layer ½-inch (1.25 cm) thick. Cut circles out of treat mixture using cookie cutter, then roll sides of each circle in toward the middle to form the cannoli shell.

4 Using a pastry bag, fill shells from both ends with ricotta mixture. Add a few of the remaining chocolate chips to each end. Serve immediately.

Treat Tip:
Make 'em ahead! You can store the filling in a covered container in the refrigerator up to 24 hours in advance. The crispy shells need to be in an airtight container at room temperature.

Choco-Dipped Crispy-Covered Sandwich Cookies

• • • • • • • • • • • • •

The name may be a mouthful, but just wait until you get one of these decadent treats in your mouth. Warning: these are highly addictive, so don't plan on eating just one!

YIELD: APPROXIMATELY 20 TREATS
TIME: 1 HOUR, PLUS 30 MINUTES
DRYING TIME
DIFFICULTY LEVEL: INTERMEDIATE

3 tbsp margarine

1 10-ounce (280 g) bag
   mini marshmallows

6 cups (150 g) crisp rice cereal

20 cream-filled chocolate
   sandwich cookies

8 ounces (225 g) chocolate
   almond bark

4 ounces (115 g) white
   almond bark

Sanding sugar or sprinkles
   (optional)

Equipment: Parchment
paper

1 Melt margarine over low heat in a 5-quart or larger saucepan. Add marshmallows, and stir. Let marshmallows melt completely, stirring occasionally. Remove from heat.

2 Stir in crisp rice cereal until covered in marshmallow. As soon as mixture is cool enough to touch, spray your hands with nonstick cooking spray and mold a thin layer of mixture around a sandwich cookie until it's completely covered (it might take a bit of practice). Set aside on parchment paper and repeat on all cookies.

3 Using a microwave-safe dish, heat 6 ounces (170 g) of chocolate almond bark in the microwave in 30-second increments until melted, stirring between each heating. (I recommend using High power level for first heating and switching to 50 percent power for subsequent heatings.) Carefully dip top half of crispy-covered cookies in chocolate, gently shaking off any excess. Return cookies to parchment paper. Melt additional chocolate almond bark as needed. Decorate with sprinkles or sugar if desired.

4 Next, using another microwave-safe dish, heat white almond bark in the microwave in 30-second increments until melted, stirring between each heating. Drizzle over chocolate-covered top of treats, and put aside until almond bark has completely set. Store in an airtight container. Best eaten within 24 hours.

Chocolate Pretzel Crispy Treat Sandwiches

· · · · · · · · · · · · · ·

These sweet-and-salty treats are a delightful twist on traditional chocolate-covered pretzels. I dare you to eat just one!

YIELD: 18 SANDWICHES
TIME: 1 HOUR
DIFFICULTY LEVEL: INTERMEDIATE

2 tbsp margarine

2¾ cups (5 ounces [140 g]) mini marshmallows

3 cups (75 g) crisp rice cereal

36 thin pretzel chips

12 ounces (340 g) chocolate almond bark or candy melts

Equipment: Parchment paper

Treat Tip:
Dipping chocolate should be thin and smooth. If it begins to get thick or clumpy, reheat it slightly and stir.

1 Melt margarine in a 3-quart or larger saucepan over low heat. Add marshmallows, and stir. Let marshmallows melt completely, stirring occasionally. Remove from heat.

2 Pour in rice cereal and stir until covered with marshmallow. Turn out onto a greased cookie sheet. With greased hands, press mix into a uniform layer, about ½ inch (1.25 cm) thick. The rice cereal mixture may not fill the entire baking sheet. Let cool.

3 Place a pretzel chip on top of the cooled rice cereal mixture. Cut around pretzel, so the crispy rice cut-out is the same size and shape as the pretzel chip. Sandwich the pretzel-shaped crispy treat between two pretzel chips. Use your fingers to shape if needed. Repeat until all sandwiches have been made.

4 Using a small, microwave-safe dish, heat half of the chocolate almond bark in the microwave in 30-second increments until completely melted, stirring between each heating. (I recommend using High power level for first heating and switching to 50 percent power for subsequent heatings.) Hold a pretzel sandwich upright and dip bottom half in melted bark, shaking off any excess. Place sandwich on a sheet of parchment paper to harden. Heat more bark as needed.

5 Store in an airtight container on countertop and serve within 24 hours.

Cosmic Crunch Cookies

A chocolate cookie plus a chocolate, caramel crunch will surely remind you of a yummy snack from your youth.

YIELD: 24 COOKIES
TIME: 45 MINUTES
DIFFICULTY LEVEL: INTERMEDIATE

1 box chocolate cake mix
2 eggs
⅓ cup (80 ml) vegetable oil
flour, for dusting
1 11-ounce (311 g) bag caramel bits
1 14-ounce (425 ml) can sweetened condensed milk
¼ cup (55 g) butter
1 12-ounce (340 g) bag chocolate chips
3 cups (75 g) crisp rice cereal

Equipment: Parchment paper, glass cup

1 Preheat oven to 375°F (190°C).

2 Line 2 baking sheets with parchment paper. Mix together cake mix, eggs, and oil with a spoon to form a dough. Roll dough into 1-inch (2.5 cm) balls and space them 2 inches (5 cm) apart on the parchment paper. Dip the bottom of a glass in flour and press balls of dough down so that they're ¼ inch (.66 cm) thick. Bake for 6 minutes. Remove from oven.

3 While cookies are baking, start making crispy topping. Melt together caramel bits, condensed milk, and butter in a saucepan over medium-high heat, stirring occasionally. Once caramel mixture has melted, add chocolate chips and stir until chips are completely melted. Remove from heat. Gently incorporate crisp rice cereal 1 cup (25 g) at a time.

4 Spread a dollop of the crispy caramel topping on one of the cookies so that top is completely covered (you may need to use your fingers to do this). Repeat for rest of cookies. Allow to cool and set. Store in an airtight container and enjoy within 2 to 3 days.

Banana Cream Pie with Crispy Vanilla Wafer Crust

This no-bake version of a banana cream pie is sure to please just as much as the real McCoy. Vanilla wafers incorporated into the crust give the dessert an extra boost of flavor.

YIELD: APPROXIMATELY 8 SLICES
TIME: 30 MINUTES ACTIVE.
30 MINUTES SETTING
DIFFICULTY LEVEL: INTERMEDIATE

Crust

2 cups vanilla wafers
2 tbsp margarine
2¾ cups (5 ounces [140 g] mini marshmallows)
1 tsp vanilla extract
3 cups (75 g) crisp rice cereal

Filling

1 3.4-ounce (96 g) package banana instant pudding mix
2 cups (475 ml) milk
2 to 3 ripe bananas
Whipped topping, thawed
8 vanilla wafers, for decoration

Equipment: 10¼-inch (26 cm) pie baking dish

1 First make the crispy treat crust. To begin, pulverize vanilla wafers in a food processor. Set aside.

2 Melt margarine over low heat in a 5-quart or larger saucepan. Add marshmallows, and stir. Let marshmallows melt completely, stirring occasionally. Add vanilla extract and ½ cup (25 g) of the vanilla wafer crumbs (there may be some leftover). Stir to combine. Remove from heat.

3 Stir in crisp rice cereal until covered with marshmallow. Turn out into 10¼-inch (26 cm) pie baking dish, making sure to press into bottom and up sides. Allow crispy crust to cool. Store covered on countertop (up to 24 hours) until ready to fill.

4 Next make the filling. In a bowl, whisk together pudding mix and milk for 2 minutes. Cover and refrigerate until set, at least 10 minutes. Keep in refrigerator until ready to use.

5 Right before serving, cut bananas into thin slices and place over crispy treat crust in a single layer, covering crust completely. Spoon pudding over the sliced bananas. Add a layer of thawed whipped topping, and decorate with vanilla wafers.

Glossary

Almond bark: This is a chocolate-like substance that, when melted, is used for dipping and drizzling. It is much easier to work with than real chocolate, which needs to be tempered (often a difficult process) when you melt it. While almond bark is similar to candy melts (see explanation below), it has the advantage of being available at the grocery store and typically costs less.

Buttercream frosting: Buttercream frosting is pretty much butter creamed together with powdered sugar. It is popular for decorating cakes, and I use it a lot to decorate my crispy treats. Check out the Buttercream Frosting recipe (page ix), where you'll learn not only how to make it, but how to use it, too.

Candy melts: These are small discs that come in a variety of colors and flavors. They are very easy to work with; you simply melt them and then dip or drizzle. Most of the time, I would recommend thinning the melted candy melts with a little vegetable shortening, as doing so results in a smoother consistency. Candy melts can be found at craft stores, cake supply stores, and some big box retailers.

Candy writers: These tubes, full of candy melts, are used for embellishing confections. Available in a variety of colors, they are great for drawing simple elements, such as a mouth or a dot for an eye. The tip doesn't really allow for fine details, though. To use, place the tube in hot water and knead until the candy inside is melted.

Decorating tip: This helpful device is a metal tip that gets affixed to the end of a piping bag. (I sometimes refer to this as an "icing tip" in the book.) Decorating tips come in all shapes and sizes. I mostly use a number 3 tip, which is great for lines. Smaller numbers— like 1, 1.5, and 2—are great for writing and fine details. The Mustache Treats (page 21) call for a number 8 tip, which has a pretty large opening for nice thick lines.

Disco dust: This very fine, nontoxic glitter adds lots of sparkle and shine to projects. There is some debate about whether or not disco dust should be eaten. If you are concerned about it, you can find food-grade glitters on the Internet. You can see the disco dust in action on the Sparkling Star Princess Wands (page 18).

Food color spray: Available at craft stores, cake supply stores, and online retailers, food color spray is a small can of aerosol food coloring. It is a great substitute for airbrushing and works well for projects like the Engagement Ring Treats (page 71) or the Pinwheel Treats (page 3) where you want only a portion of something colored. I especially like the silver, gold, and pearl sprays—the look they give is not easily attained with regular food colorings. Make sure to shake well before using, and protect a large area from over-spray. Food color spray is permanent, and it will stain.

Gel food coloring: Gel colorings are highly superior to the liquid food coloring that is available at the grocery store. They come in a large variety of colors, including black and white. They are thick and won't water down your creations. They are also a lot stronger, so a little bit of gel coloring will go a long way. Craft stores usually have some colors, but for a wider selection, I recommend finding a specialist cake supply store or ordering online.

Piping bag: These bags are intended to be filled with frosting and used to decorate cakes, cookies, and in this case, crispy treats. See the Buttercream Frosting recipe (page ix) for instructions on how to use a piping bag.

Quins: These edible embellishments are basically shaped sprinkles, available in all sorts of forms, such as bats for Halloween, pink ribbons for breast cancer awareness, or even crayons for a touch of whimsy. They come in basic circles, as well. The Birthday Hat Treats (page 67), for example, use jumbo circle quins.

Turbinado sugar: This sugar is brown in color and has large crystals. It gets the name turbinado because the sugar is spun in a turbine during the manufacturing process. The brown color naturally comes from the sugar cane, whereas traditional brown sugar is white sugar with molasses added. Turbinado sugar should be stored in a cool, dry place inside an airtight container to prevent hardening.

Ingredient Alternatives

Cooking for others can be difficult given the prevalence of various dietary issues, such as food allergies, sensitivities, and preferences, just to name a few. I've compiled a list of some common food-related problems and suggestions for ingredient substitutions.

Diabetic-friendly: Sugar-free marshmallows can be purchased from upscale grocery stores. Before serving any low- or no-sugar treats to someone who is diabetic, be sure to clear all of the ingredients with that individual first.

Dye-free: Some kids and adults are sensitive to particular food dyes. Marshmallows actually contain a blue dye to help them look a brighter white. Once again, upscale grocery stores will often have you covered with marshmallows that are dye-free. Just make sure you check the labels.

Gluten-free: Even though crisp rice cereal is rice-based, it often contains an ingredient (malt, for example) that is not gluten-free, or the cereal simply isn't certified gluten-free. Several brands, however, do make specific gluten-free versions—just be sure to read the labels and ingredients carefully. Health-food stores usually carry gluten-free version if you're unable to find them at your regular grocery store.

Nut allergies: Ingredients for standard crispy treats do not contain any nut allergy warnings. Be sure to check the labels of any additional ingredients. Peanut butter is a popular ingredient in sweets. My favorite peanut butter substitute is cookie butter; it has the same texture as peanut butter and tastes delicious.

Vegan: Coconut oil or soy margarine is a great substitute for the traditional margarine called for in crispy treat recipes. Unfortunately, marshmallows also tend to contain gelatin, which is an animal product. I have found that there are multiple brands of vegan marshmallows. Check out your local health-minded grocery stores to find them.